The
SAGITTARIUS
Path

YOUR DAILY 2026 HOROSCOPE GUIDE

AMANDA M CLARKE

Copyright © Amanda M Clarke 2026
KORU Publishing

All rights reserved. All content, materials, and intellectual property in this book or any other platform owned by Koru Publishing are protected by copyright laws. This includes text, images, graphics, videos, audio, software, and any other form of content that may be produced by Koru Publishing.

No part of this content may be reproduced, distributed, or transmitted in any form or by any means without the prior written permission of Koru Publishing. This means that you cannot copy, reproduce, or use any of the content in this book for commercial or personal purposes without the express written consent of Koru Publishing.

Unauthorized use of any copyrighted material owned by Koru Publishing may result in legal action being taken against you. Koru Publishing reserves the right to pursue all available legal remedies against any individual or entity found to be infringing on its copyright.

In summary, Koru Publishing © 2024 holds exclusive rights to all the content produced by it, and any unauthorized use of such content will result in legal action.

KORU Publishing

KORU (Maori:NZ)
A symbol of spiritual growth and spiritual connection.

Rocky Point Townhouse, CHRISTMAS ISLAND, Western Australia 6798

ISBN: 978-1-923614-09-3

More on the Bookshelves at
www.theliteraryoracle.com

Disclaimer: The Sagittarius Path: Your daily 2026 horoscope guide book provides information on astrological readings and intuative interpretations, it is not intended as a substitute for professional advice, diagnosis, or treatment. The information contained in this book is provided for educational and entertainment purposes only and is not meant to be taken as specific advice for individual circumstances. The author and publisher make no representations or warranties with respect to the accuracy or completeness of the contents of this book and specifically disclaim any implied warranties of merchantability or fitness for a particular purpose. The reader should always consult with a licensed professional for any specific concerns or questions. The author and publisher shall not be liable for any loss or damage caused or alleged to have been caused, directly or indirectly, by the information contained in this book. The use of this book is at the reader's sole risk

More from Amanda Clarke
The Literary Oracle
www.theliteracyoracle.com

The "Daily Guidance" series offers an innovative approach to finding spiritual wisdom and practical advice. Each book in the series is a unique tool designed for daily introspection and decision-making. Readers are invited to meditate on a question or seek general guidance for the day, then flip to a random page in the book. The page they land on provides a personalized message from various spiritual sources, such as angels, tarot, or spirit animals. With each turn of the page, these books deliver insightful, positive messages and mantras to inspire personal growth and provide clarity on life's daily challenges and decisions.

Other books in this series:-
The Angelic Oracles
Daily Angel Tarot Reading
Mystic Tarot Cat
Oracle of the Tarot Cat
Vibes Unveiled
Spirit Animal Oracle
Answers from the Oracles
Messages from the Angels

Supporting Indie Authors

Love your daily guidance? You can grab more of my books direct from The Literary Oracle: www.theliteraryoracle.com

Buying direct means:
- Much better prices for you + free shipping.
- More support for me as an indie author
- More magical books in your hands

My books are also available worldwide through online bookstores, but direct purchases help keep the magic flowing.

Thank you for supporting indie creativity!

Scan me

Welcome to The Sagittarius Path: Your Daily 2026 Horoscope Guide — your bold, truth-seeking companion for the year ahead. Crafted for the adventurous, optimistic, and endlessly curious Sagittarius, this guide honours the way you move through life — with open horizons, an untamed spirit, and a fiery heart that craves freedom and meaning in equal measure.

Inside, you'll find daily horoscopes paired with gratitude designed to align with your natural strengths. Each entry is here to support you through 2026 with guidance that speaks directly to your adventurous soul — whether you're chasing opportunities in your career, expanding your knowledge, deepening connections, or simply following where your restless spirit leads.

This isn't about holding back — it's about alignment. As you turn these pages, you'll receive encouragement, clarity, and cosmic reminders to trust your instincts, embrace growth, and honour your path. Let this be the year you explore boldly, laugh loudly, and step fully into the life you were born to live — guided always by your fire, your wisdom, and the stars above.

The Answers You Seek

Are Within

January 2026

Sagittarius
01 January 2026

The year opens with a spark of optimism, Sagittarius. The Sun aligns with Mercury, lighting up your communication zone. Your words carry weight and influence today—whether spoken, written, or even whispered. People look to you for wisdom, so speak with clarity and truth. This is a perfect time to journal your intentions, send a meaningful message, or start conversations that matter. Trust that the universe amplifies your voice. Begin this year with purpose.

Gratitude Mantra

I am grateful for my voice and the power it has to inspire, connect, and create new beginnings.

Sagittarius
02 January 2026

Venus highlights your finances, reminding you to balance indulgence with practicality. Your generous spirit sometimes spends first, thinks later, but today's cosmic nudge asks you to consider long-term goals. Where can you invest in yourself wisely? Look at your budget not as restriction but as empowerment. Treat yourself, but remember that security brings freedom too. Balance is the keyword—spend with joy but plan with wisdom.

Gratitude Mantra

I am grateful for the resources I have and the wisdom to manage them with joy and purpose.

Sagittarius
03 January 2026

The Moon moves through your adventurous ninth house, calling you to explore new ideas, cultures, or philosophies. You're restless today, craving expansion beyond the ordinary. Whether it's booking travel, diving into a new subject, or simply seeing your daily routine differently, growth comes through curiosity. Trust that stepping outside your comfort zone creates opportunities for the future. Stretch your mind as much as your body.

Gratitude Mantra

I am grateful for the adventures ahead, knowing every new step brings wisdom, joy, and fresh perspective.

Sagittarius
04 January 2026

Today's planetary energy turns your focus inward, Sagittarius. The Moon highlights reflection and self-care. While you prefer action, taking time to pause strengthens you. Look at what patterns from last year no longer serve you. Release what feels heavy. Your natural fire burns brighter when unburdened. Use meditation, journaling, or a long walk to clear mental clutter. Recharging now prepares you for bold leaps ahead.

Gratitude Mantra

I release what no longer serves me and give thanks for the space to grow into new beginnings.

Sagittarius
05 January 2026

The Sun harmonizes with Uranus, sparking unexpected changes in your daily routine. Something may shift suddenly—a plan cancels, a new idea appears, or work takes a surprising turn. Instead of resisting, embrace flexibility. You thrive in spontaneity, and today the universe tests your ability to adapt. Trust the detour; it may open a path far better than the one you planned.

Gratitude Mantra

I am grateful for life's surprises, knowing they often lead me exactly where I'm meant to go.

Sagittarius
06 January 2026

The Moon in your sign makes you magnetic today. People notice your enthusiasm, charm, and spark. This is an excellent day to share your vision, pitch ideas, or simply let your authentic self shine. Confidence flows naturally, but remember humility keeps you relatable. Your optimism inspires others more than you know. Let your fire guide not just your path but brighten others' journeys too.

Gratitude Mantra

I am grateful for the fire within me that lights my path and inspires those around me.

Sagittarius
07 January 2026

Saturn steadies your communication zone today, urging patience and responsibility in how you speak. Your words can build or break bridges now, so choose carefully. If there's a difficult conversation you've avoided, this is the day to approach it with honesty and respect. Your natural bluntness, softened with compassion, becomes your superpower. Speak truth but also listen deeply.

Gratitude Mantra

I am grateful for the wisdom to speak with honesty and compassion, strengthening my connections with others.

Sagittarius
8 January 2026

The Moon highlights your second house of values and money. Today's energy is about recognising your worth—not just financially but personally. If you've been underestimating your talents, the cosmos reminds you that your skills and knowledge have real value. This is a good day to revisit financial goals, consider side opportunities, or simply demand fair recognition for what you bring to the table. Stand tall and know your worth.

Gratitude Mantra

I am grateful for my unique talents and the value they bring to both my life and others.

Sagittarius
9 January 2026

Mars fuels your communication zone, giving you boldness in speech and thought. You're quick-witted, fiery, and passionate today. Be mindful—your words can either spark inspiration or conflict. Channel this energy into constructive conversations, presentations, or creative writing rather than arguments. When you speak with intention, your message carries immense power. Let your fire light the way but not scorch bridges.

Gratitude Mantra

I am grateful for the courage to express myself clearly and passionately, while also choosing kindness in my words.

Sagittarius
10 January 2026

With the Sun square Neptune, your energy feels scattered. Plans may blur, details slip, or confusion surrounds a situation. Don't force clarity—accept the haze. Use the day for spiritual reflection, creative pursuits, or rest instead of rigid schedules. Avoid overpromising, as misunderstandings could arise. Trust that fog will clear, and patience today will prevent regret tomorrow. Flow with the rhythm, not against it.

Gratitude Mantra

I am grateful for the chance to pause, reflect, and trust that clarity will come in divine timing.

Sagittarius
11 January 2026

The Moon in Aquarius sparks originality and vision. Ideas pop like fireworks, and your ability to think outside the box shines. Group settings or brainstorming with friends may bring surprising breakthroughs. This is a day to trust your eccentric side—what feels unconventional may be exactly what's needed. Don't hold back your unique perspective; your voice adds magic to conversations and projects.

Gratitude Mantra

I am grateful for my originality and the freedom to share my ideas with courage and authenticity.

Sagittarius
12 January 2026

Jupiter, your ruling planet, aligns harmoniously with Venus today, bringing joy, luck, and warmth to relationships. Whether love, friendship, or family, connections feel expansive. It's a beautiful day for celebration, romance, or deep conversation. Opportunities to meet new people or rekindle bonds may appear. Your natural optimism attracts blessings, and you'll find others drawn to your energy. Love and abundance flow freely.

Gratitude Mantra

I am grateful for the love, joy, and abundance that flow effortlessly into my relationships and daily life.

Sagittarius
13 January 2026

A strong focus on your career zone emerges. The Sun's energy reminds you that success requires consistent effort, not just bursts of passion. You may be called to prove yourself or step into a leadership role. Don't shy away; you're more capable than you realise. Long-term goals need your attention now—lay solid foundations for the future. The universe supports your ambition.

Gratitude Mantra

I am grateful for the discipline and vision that guide me toward lasting success and meaningful achievements.

Sagittarius
14 January 2026

Today brings grounding energy as the Moon highlights stability and routine. It's a day to tend to the basics—health, habits, and home. While not as thrilling as adventures, these simple rituals fuel your fire in the long run. A small shift in diet, exercise, or organisation today has ripple effects for months. Honour the small steps—they build big dreams.

Gratitude Mantra

I am grateful for the strength found in simple routines and the stability that supports my bigger adventures.

Sagittarius
15 January 2026

With the Moon lighting up your creative zone, today is about passion projects and play. Your imagination runs wild, and inspiration finds you in surprising ways—through music, art, or even casual conversations. Don't ignore those sparks. Create something, no matter how small. Your playful energy also draws others toward you, making social interactions fun and uplifting. Tap into your inner child—joy itself is a powerful form of wisdom.

Gratitude Mantra

I am grateful for the creative sparks that flow through me, reminding me that joy is my natural state.

Sagittarius
16 January 2026

Mars harmonises with Saturn, giving you the discipline to channel your fiery drive into practical results. You often prefer freedom over structure, Sagittarius, but today the cosmos shows you the strength in focused effort. Tackle a big task or take steps toward long-term goals. Your energy is steady, not fleeting, making it easier to build momentum. Success today comes from patience paired with passion.

Gratitude Mantra

I am grateful for the balance of energy and discipline that helps me build the future I desire.

Sagittarius
17 January 2026

The Moon in your partnership sector brings relationships into focus. A heart-to-heart conversation could shift dynamics in a powerful way. Whether with a friend, lover, or colleague, honesty paves the way forward. Don't rush or avoid vulnerable truths—your sincerity is a gift. This is a day to listen as much as you speak. Mutual respect builds lasting connections now.

Gratitude Mantra

I am grateful for the people in my life and the openness that allows our bonds to deepen with trust.

Sagittarius
18 January 2026

Neptune's influence heightens intuition today. Pay attention to dreams, gut feelings, and subtle signs. Logic may not reveal all answers—your inner compass does. Avoid being swept away by illusions or wishful thinking, but allow your imagination to guide your steps. A spiritual practice or creative outlet will help channel this energy productively. You're more connected to unseen realms than usual—listen closely.

Gratitude Mantra

I am grateful for my intuition and the unseen guidance that leads me with gentle wisdom.

Sagittarius
19 January 2026

The Sun moves into Aquarius, shifting your focus to friendships, networking, and shared ideas. Your social circle becomes a source of inspiration and opportunity. Be open to collaboration—someone in your orbit may have a key piece to your next adventure. Group energy fuels you now, reminding you that no dream is achieved alone. Say yes to invitations, even spontaneous ones.

Gratitude Mantra

I am grateful for the connections that expand my world and the people who bring energy and vision into my life.

Sagittarius
20 January 2026

With the Moon energising your work sector, attention to detail matters today. You may feel pulled toward getting things organised, fixing mistakes, or fine-tuning projects. Though it's not glamorous, this focus creates clarity and space for future growth. Treat your daily responsibilities as sacred—every small act contributes to your bigger vision. Dedication pays off in unseen ways.

Gratitude Mantra

I am grateful for the clarity that comes from tending to details, knowing they build the foundation for success.

Sagittarius
21 January 2026

A powerful alignment between Venus and Pluto stirs transformation in relationships and finances. Something deep may surface—truths about intimacy, money, or power dynamics. While intensity can feel overwhelming, facing it honestly leads to liberation. Don't shy away from uncomfortable conversations; they are doorways to growth. What feels like an ending may actually be the start of something more authentic.

Gratitude Mantra

I am grateful for the strength to embrace transformation and the wisdom to allow endings to open new doors.

Sagittarius
22 January 2026

The Moon highlights your zone of dreams and spirituality today. You may feel more sensitive, intuitive, and reflective. It's a good day to rest, meditate, or journal your inner thoughts. Don't push for external progress; instead, tend to your inner world. Insights from dreams or quiet moments may guide your next steps. Pay attention to subtle synchronicities—they're messages meant just for you.

Gratitude Mantra

I am grateful for the quiet moments that connect me to my inner wisdom and guide my future choices.

Sagittarius
23 January 2026

A burst of energy arrives as the Moon enters your sign. Suddenly, the world feels more vibrant, and you're ready to take action. People notice your enthusiasm and may look to you for direction. Take advantage of this momentum—start a new project, make a bold decision, or simply show up authentically. Your fire is magnetic and contagious.

Gratitude Mantra

I am grateful for my natural enthusiasm and the energy it brings to everything I touch.

Sagittarius
24 January 2026

Mercury aligns with Jupiter, expanding your thoughts and communication. This is a perfect day for learning, teaching, or sharing your ideas widely. Your words carry optimism and wisdom, opening doors to new opportunities. Travel plans, publishing projects, or long-term studies may also come into focus. Think big, Sagittarius—your mind is a powerful tool for growth and influence.

Gratitude Mantra

I am grateful for my expanding mind and the opportunities my words create for learning, teaching, and inspiring others.

Sagittarius
25 January 2026

With the Moon in your sign, emotions run strong today. You may feel torn between independence and connection. While your fiery spirit craves freedom, relationships may demand attention. The key is balance—honour your needs while respecting others'. This is also a day for self-expression, so speak your truth without apology. Authenticity keeps bonds strong.

Gratitude Mantra

I am grateful for the courage to honour both my freedom and the relationships that enrich my journey.

Sagittarius
26 January 2026

Today's energy is practical as the Moon enters Capricorn, pushing you to focus on career, finances, and long-term goals. You may feel determined to get serious about building stability. Use this grounded energy to review budgets, plan projects, or make progress at work. What you begin today can bring steady results in months to come.

Gratitude Mantra

I am grateful for the determination and focus that help me build a stable and prosperous future.

Sagittarius
27 January 2026

The Moon in Capricorn reminds you of responsibility, but Uranus stirs surprises. Plans may suddenly shift, demanding quick adaptation. Don't resist—flexibility is your strength. What looks like an obstacle may actually push you into a better direction. Stay calm, adjust, and trust that the universe has your back. Your adventurous nature thrives when life takes unexpected turns.

Gratitude Mantra

I am grateful for my ability to adapt quickly and find opportunity in life's sudden changes.

Sagittarius
28 January 2026

Venus moves into a harmonious aspect with Jupiter, blessing relationships, finances, and personal joy. This is one of those rare cosmic days where everything seems to flow easily. Connections feel warmer, opportunities arise, and abundance feels closer. Don't overindulge, but do allow yourself to enjoy life's sweetness. Share your joy with others—it doubles when spread.

Gratitude Mantra

I am grateful for the abundance of love, joy, and opportunities flowing into my life with ease.

Sagittarius
29 January 2026

The Moon highlights friendships and group dynamics, Sagittarius. Today you may feel pulled to spend time with like-minded souls. Collaboration, teamwork, or networking brings surprising inspiration. Don't underestimate the power of shared ideas—someone in your circle could spark a breakthrough for you. Your role may be to lead, encourage, or simply bring your fire to the group. Trust in the energy of community.

Gratitude Mantra

I am grateful for the friendships and connections that inspire me and help me grow in unexpected ways.

Sagittarius
30 January 2026

With Mercury squaring Uranus, plans may twist suddenly. Conversations could take unexpected turns, or new information may alter your perspective. Stay open, adaptable, and lighthearted. If you meet resistance, try humour instead of frustration. Surprises today test your flexibility but also bring exciting insights. What first feels disruptive may actually liberate you from limitations you hadn't noticed.

Gratitude Mantra

I am grateful for life's surprises and my ability to stay flexible, turning challenges into opportunities for growth.

Sagittarius
31 January 2026

The Moon shifts into Pisces, drawing your focus toward home, family, and emotional roots. You may feel the urge to cocoon, reflect, or nurture your inner world. Family interactions may carry extra meaning now, helping you heal old wounds or strengthen bonds. If solitude calls, honour it—you recharge by tending to the heart as much as the mind.

Gratitude Mantra

I am grateful for the love and healing that flows from home, family, and time spent in reflection.

February 2026

Sagittarius
01 February 2026

The Sun and Saturn align, urging you to take responsibility for long-term goals. Today feels serious, yet productive. Don't shy away from commitments—you're building something meaningful that requires structure and discipline. This may involve career, education, or financial matters. It's not a day for shortcuts, but the effort you put in now secures lasting success.

Gratitude Mantra

I am grateful for the discipline and commitment that guide me toward my long-term goals and ambitions.

Sagittarius
02 February 2026

The Moon in Pisces stirs deep emotions, while Neptune amplifies your imagination. Creative or spiritual activities are highly favoured today. However, avoid over-idealising situations or ignoring practical details. Ground your dreams in reality by taking one small step forward. You can merge vision with action if you pace yourself wisely. Use your sensitivity as a compass.

Gratitude Mantra

I am grateful for my imagination and intuition, which guide me gently toward inspired and purposeful action.

Sagittarius
03 February 2026

As the Moon enters Aries, energy turns fiery and bold again. This is a day to act, initiate, or take risks. Your adventurous spirit feels reignited, and opportunities to stand out appear. Confidence is high, but watch impatience—it could trip you up. Channel this surge of energy into something productive that aligns with your bigger dreams.

Gratitude Mantra

I am grateful for my courage and the fire that pushes me to act boldly and with passion.

Sagittarius
04 February 2026

A harmonious Venus aspect boosts charm and attraction. Love, friendships, and finances benefit under this influence. You may receive recognition, compliments, or unexpected generosity. Today flows with ease, so enjoy it—indulge in a treat, connect with loved ones, or appreciate simple pleasures. Your optimism and warmth attract abundance, proving joy itself is magnetic.

Gratitude Mantra

I am grateful for the love and abundance that surrounds me, and for the joy I both give and receive.

Sagittarius
5 February 2026

The Moon highlights stability, nudging you to focus on practical matters like health, routines, and organisation. You may feel a strong urge to simplify and streamline your environment. Clearing clutter, creating schedules, or refining habits will give you a sense of control. Remember, Sagittarius, small changes made consistently shape the bigger picture. Honour the details today, even if they don't feel exciting—they'll support your freedom later.

Gratitude Mantra

I am grateful for the strength found in small, steady actions that build stability and freedom in my life.

Sagittarius
6 February 2026

Mercury trines Pluto, sharpening your insight and helping you cut through illusions. Conversations may take on a deeper tone, revealing hidden truths. You have the ability to influence others with your words today, but honesty is the foundation. Don't shy away from sensitive topics—your courage to speak openly inspires others. It's also a powerful day for research, journaling, or diving into mysteries.

Gratitude Mantra

I am grateful for my sharp insight and the courage to speak truth that empowers both myself and others.

Sagittarius
7 February 2026

The Moon in Taurus highlights pleasure, beauty, and comfort. Today invites you to slow down and indulge in life's sensual joys. Good food, music, nature, or simply rest brings healing. While you usually chase adventure, don't underestimate the wisdom of stillness. Pleasure isn't laziness—it's replenishment. Let your senses guide you, reminding you that joy is a form of medicine too.

Gratitude Mantra

I am grateful for life's simple pleasures and the way they restore balance to my body, mind, and soul.

Sagittarius
8 February 2026

A lively energy stirs as Venus aligns with Mars, igniting passion and enthusiasm. Relationships may feel magnetic, creativity flows easily, and your charm is undeniable. This is a day to take bold steps toward love or creative pursuits. Your fiery spirit draws attention, and opportunities may open through sheer charisma. Don't overdo it—channel this energy into something meaningful.

Gratitude Mantra

I am grateful for the passion and enthusiasm that fuel my connections and creative expressions.

Sagittarius
9 February 2026

With the Moon in Gemini, your mind is buzzing with curiosity. Conversations, learning, and new ideas dominate the day. You may feel pulled in many directions—don't let overwhelm steal your spark. Focus on variety without overcommitting. Social interactions bring insight and inspiration now, so keep your schedule open for spontaneous connections. Embrace the joy of exploration.

Gratitude Mantra

I am grateful for my curious mind and the inspiration that comes from exploring new ideas and connections.

Sagittarius
10 February 2026

The Moon continues in Gemini, squaring Neptune, which may create confusion or misunderstandings. Be careful with details, contracts, or promises today. You're brimming with ideas, but clarity is needed before action. Don't rush decisions—pause, review, and wait for the fog to lift. Instead, use the dreamy energy for creative work or spiritual reflection. Trust that clarity will return.

Gratitude Mantra

I am grateful for my ability to pause, reflect, and allow clarity to arrive before I take action.

Sagittarius
11 February 2026

The Moon moves into Cancer, drawing your attention to emotional connections and self-nurturing. You may feel more sensitive than usual, craving comfort and reassurance. It's a day to strengthen bonds with loved ones or tend to your own heart. Home and family matters may take priority now. Honour your need for rest and emotional replenishment—you'll feel stronger tomorrow.

Gratitude Mantra

I am grateful for the comfort of emotional connections and the healing power of nurturing myself and loved ones.

Sagittarius
12 February 2026

Today's Cancer Moon emphasizes emotional security and family matters. You may feel pulled between independence and the comfort of belonging. Old feelings could resurface, giving you the chance to heal. Nurture both yourself and those closest to you. Cooking a meal, tidying your space, or sharing stories with loved ones brings grounding. Remember, Sagittarius, emotional strength fuels your adventurous spirit just as much as freedom does.

Gratitude Mantra

I am grateful for the love and emotional grounding that family, home, and heartfelt connections bring to my life.

Sagittarius
13 February 2026

Venus in harmony with Neptune stirs compassion and creativity. Your heart feels wide open today, inspiring acts of kindness, generosity, or artistry. Music, poetry, or spiritual practices may move you deeply. Romance is highlighted, but in a soulful, tender way. Let your softer side shine—you'll find it draws others close. Release expectations and allow magic to flow naturally.

Gratitude Mantra

I am grateful for the compassion and creativity flowing through me, touching others and reminding me of life's magic.

Sagittarius
14 February 2026

Valentine's Day feels extra meaningful as cosmic energy highlights love and partnership. Whether partnered or single, today is about celebrating connection—romantic, platonic, or self-love. Express affection openly, Sagittarius, and let people know they matter. Surprises in relationships may occur, but they bring honesty and clarity. Love is a journey, not a destination. Celebrate where you are right now.

Gratitude Mantra

I am grateful for the love in my life, in all its forms, and for the joy of giving and receiving.

Sagittarius
15 February 2026

The Moon in Leo fuels your adventurous and playful side. This is a perfect day to seek joy through creativity, travel, or fun experiences. Your charisma shines, making it easier to win people over or inspire them with your vision. Take the lead where others hesitate. Your confidence sets the tone, and doors open when you act boldly.

Gratitude Mantra

I am grateful for my adventurous spirit and the confidence to step boldly into opportunities that light me up.

Sagittarius
16 February 2026

A practical influence arrives as Mercury aligns with Saturn. Conversations and plans may feel serious, but they bring stability and focus. Today is excellent for making long-term agreements, contracts, or commitments. Your words carry authority, so use them wisely. If you've been procrastinating on decisions, now's the time to get clear. Small, steady steps secure the future.

Gratitude Mantra

I am grateful for the clarity and discipline that help me make wise, long-lasting decisions.

Sagittarius
17 February 2026

The Moon highlights career matters, shining a light on your ambitions. Recognition or responsibility may come your way, testing your readiness to step up. Don't shy from the spotlight—your natural leadership is needed. Trust in your ability to manage challenges without losing your optimism. Hard work today builds respect and opens pathways toward bigger opportunities.

Gratitude Mantra

I am grateful for the recognition of my efforts and the courage to step into leadership with confidence.

Sagittarius
18 February 2026

The Sun enters Pisces, shifting your focus toward home, rest, and emotional nourishment. This is a month to tend to your roots and inner world. Slow down enough to listen to what your soul craves. Home projects, family connections, or simply retreating from the busyness will refresh you. Remember, Sagittarius, even explorers need a safe haven to return to.

Gratitude Mantra

I am grateful for the peace and restoration that comes from creating a sanctuary within my home and heart.

Sagittarius
19 February 2026

The Pisces Moon highlights rest and healing, Sagittarius. You may feel more emotional than usual, sensing the moods of those around you. Don't ignore this sensitivity—use it as a compass. Creative or spiritual practices bring comfort today. Avoid overcommitting, as your energy needs replenishing. This is a perfect evening for candles, music, or simply quiet reflection. Protect your energy and allow space to recharge.

Gratitude Mantra

I am grateful for the healing that comes when I slow down, listen inward, and honour my emotional needs.

Sagittarius
20 February 2026

With Mars energising your daily routines, you feel the push to get things done. Productivity soars, but be careful not to scatter your fire across too many tasks. Focus on one or two priorities and watch them unfold beautifully. Physical activity is favoured—exercise, dance, or movement will keep your energy flowing. Use this drive wisely, Sagittarius.

Gratitude Mantra

I am grateful for the energy and motivation that help me complete tasks and strengthen my daily routines.

Sagittarius
21 February 2026

The Moon in Aries brings a burst of passion and courage. You're bold, spontaneous, and ready to take risks. This is an excellent day for new beginnings—projects, adventures, or even love. Your enthusiasm is infectious, drawing others to your vision. Be mindful of impulsiveness, but don't let fear stop you. Bold action leads to breakthroughs now.

Gratitude Mantra

I am grateful for the courage to take bold steps that align with my adventurous spirit and dreams.

Sagittarius
22 February 2026

Venus aligns with Pluto, stirring intensity in relationships or finances. Deep truths may surface, pushing you to confront patterns that no longer serve. It's a day of transformation—sometimes uncomfortable, but ultimately freeing. Face emotions honestly, Sagittarius, and you'll come out lighter and stronger. Endings may pave the way for beginnings, so trust the process.

Gratitude Mantra

I am grateful for the strength to face transformation and the wisdom to let go of what no longer serves me.

Sagittarius
23 February 2026

The Moon in Taurus steadies your energy, bringing calm after recent intensity. Today is perfect for grounding yourself with nature, routine, or simple pleasures. Focus on what feels solid and secure. Financial matters also benefit from attention now—review budgets, set goals, or plan for the long term. Slow, steady energy wins the race.

Gratitude Mantra

I am grateful for the grounding energy that steadies me and supports my path toward security and abundance.

Sagittarius
24 February 2026

A Full Moon in Virgo highlights health, work, and balance. Something you've been juggling may come to a head, pushing you to adjust routines. This is a time of release—let go of habits or tasks that drain you. Embrace healthier rhythms that allow both productivity and freedom. The cosmos reminds you that balance is your superpower now.

Gratitude Mantra

I am grateful for the clarity to release old habits and embrace balance in my daily life.

Sagittarius
25 February 2026

The Moon in Virgo continues to fine-tune your routines. Today brings a practical energy for organisation, planning, and tending to details. It's a good time for decluttering, simplifying, or completing unfinished work. While you prefer big visions, Sagittarius, the universe reminds you that small steps sustain big dreams. Honour the details—they carry hidden magic.

Gratitude Mantra

I am grateful for the order and organisation that help me stay aligned with my bigger goals.

Sagittarius
26 February 2026

The Libra Moon highlights partnerships, urging balance in give-and-take. You may feel called to compromise or restore harmony in a relationship. Avoid extremes—seek common ground where both sides feel seen. Conversations flow best when honesty is softened with empathy. You don't need to lose independence to maintain connection. Sagittarius, your wisdom helps guide relationships into greater fairness and mutual respect today.

Gratitude Mantra

I am grateful for the harmony created when I honour both my independence and the connections that enrich my life.

Sagittarius
27 February 2026

Mercury aligns with Uranus, sparking sudden insights and breakthroughs. Ideas may arrive like lightning, showing you new solutions or directions. Keep your mind open and flexible—what feels unconventional could be brilliant. Communication today may feel surprising, but refreshing. Take notes, brainstorm, or explore creative outlets. Innovation thrives now, and your adventurous mind is primed to grasp it.

Gratitude Mantra

I am grateful for fresh ideas and the inspiration that strikes when I least expect it.

Sagittarius
28 February 2026

The Moon in Libra continues to highlight relationships, while Venus encourages warmth and affection. This is an excellent day to reconnect with loved ones, strengthen bonds, or enjoy romantic moments. If single, you may meet someone intriguing through social settings or shared interests. Love and harmony flow easily today—lean into joy and connection.

Gratitude Mantra

I am grateful for the love and connection that flows into my relationships, bringing warmth and joy.

March
2026

Sagittarius
01 March 2026

The Moon enters Scorpio, intensifying emotions and intuition. Secrets may surface, or you might feel a deep pull to reflect inward. This is a powerful day for transformation, releasing old fears, and trusting your instincts. Don't shy away from emotional truths—they hold keys to your freedom. What feels intense now will ultimately empower you.

Gratitude Mantra

I am grateful for the strength that comes from facing truth and the transformation that follows.

Sagittarius
02 March 2026

Mars energises your zone of creativity and self-expression, urging you to take bold action. Whether artistic, romantic, or adventurous, your fire blazes brightly. Don't hold back—share your passions openly. Others will be inspired by your courage. Be mindful not to dominate, but let your enthusiasm uplift. Today favours starting projects that need passion and persistence.

Gratitude Mantra

I am grateful for my passion and the courage to express it freely and boldly.

Sagittarius
03 March 2026

The Moon in Scorpio makes this a deeply intuitive day. You may sense what others don't say, guiding you in relationships and decisions. It's a good day for research, reflection, or healing old wounds. Your natural honesty combined with insight helps you cut through illusions. Trust your gut—it's sharper than usual now.

Gratitude Mantra

I am grateful for my intuition and the clarity it brings when words or actions fall short.

Sagittarius
4 March 2026

The Sagittarius Moon returns, lifting your spirit and recharging your adventurous heart. Optimism flows, and you feel ready to stretch into new horizons. Travel, learning, or bold opportunities may appear. Share your wisdom and humour—people are drawn to your lightness. Trust your vision and act with faith; doors are opening now. Your fire feels unstoppable today.

Gratitude Mantra

I am grateful for my optimism and the courage to embrace new horizons with joy and faith.

Sagittarius
5 March 2026

With the Moon in your sign, your confidence and optimism shine brightly today. You're eager to explore, share ideas, and connect with others. Use this expansive energy to take the first step toward a project you've been dreaming about. Your enthusiasm is magnetic, but remember to stay grounded and finish what you start. The universe is backing your boldness now, so don't let self-doubt dim your fire.

Gratitude Mantra

I am grateful for my adventurous spirit and the courage to take bold steps toward my dreams.

Sagittarius
6 March 2026

The Moon shifts into Capricorn, grounding your fiery energy. Today is about discipline, structure, and steady progress. While spontaneity feels more natural to you, Sagittarius, this cosmic push asks you to commit to your responsibilities. Long-term success comes from patience, not just bursts of enthusiasm. Focus on practical steps, organisation, and follow-through. This is the day to lay foundations that will support your freedom later.

Gratitude Mantra

I am grateful for the discipline that strengthens me and helps me build a future aligned with my vision.

Sagittarius
7 March 2026

Mercury harmonises with Jupiter, expanding your mind and sharpening communication. Your words hold influence today, and opportunities for learning, teaching, or publishing are highlighted. This is an excellent day to share your ideas with a wider audience, whether through writing, presenting, or casual conversations. Your optimism inspires others, and new doors may open through networking. Think big, Sagittarius—this is your time to voice your truth.

Gratitude Mantra

I am grateful for my voice and the opportunities it creates to share wisdom and inspire others.

Sagittarius
8 March 2026

The Moon in Capricorn continues to spotlight responsibility and achievement. You may feel tested today by challenges that require persistence and maturity. Resist the temptation to rush—steady focus brings success. Conversations around career, finances, or authority figures may arise, but you are more capable than you think. This is a day to prove reliability without losing your natural spark. Balance seriousness with your trademark optimism.

Gratitude Mantra

I am grateful for my resilience and the strength to handle responsibilities with both determination and optimism.

Sagittarius
9 March 2026

The Moon enters Aquarius, sparking curiosity, innovation, and social energy. You're drawn to friends, groups, and ideas that expand your worldview. Collaboration may bring exciting breakthroughs, so share your perspective freely. You may feel restless under routine, so shake things up with something new. Unconventional solutions work best today, and your ability to think outside the box is your greatest gift.

Gratitude Mantra

I am grateful for my curiosity and the innovative ideas that help me grow and inspire those around me.

Sagittarius
10 March 2026

Venus aligns with Jupiter, creating one of the luckiest and most joyful days of the month. Relationships sparkle, opportunities arise, and abundance feels within reach. This is a day to celebrate love, friendship, and the simple pleasures of life. Say yes to invitations, explore creative outlets, and trust that the universe is smiling on you. Your natural optimism magnifies this cosmic blessing—enjoy it fully.

Gratitude Mantra

I am grateful for the love, joy, and abundance that flow freely into my life today.

Sagittarius
11 March 2026

The Moon in Aquarius keeps your focus on community and big ideas, but Saturn reminds you to be realistic. Dreams are wonderful, but today calls for planning how to bring them into reality. Don't fear structure—it's the bridge between inspiration and achievement. Your wisdom lies in balancing vision with practicality. By blending optimism with discipline, you'll create results that last.

Gratitude Mantra

I am grateful for the balance of vision and practicality that allows my dreams to take root and flourish.

Sagittarius
12 March 2026

The Moon moves into Pisces, turning your focus inward toward home, rest, and emotional replenishment. You may feel more sensitive today, craving comfort and security. This is an ideal time to step back from the noise of the outside world and reconnect with your inner sanctuary. Family or home projects may call for attention, but keep the pace gentle. Listen to your intuition—it's strong now. Sagittarius, even explorers need rest stops along the way.

Gratitude Mantra

I am grateful for the quiet spaces that allow me to restore my energy and listen to my heart.

Sagittarius
13 March 2026

The Pisces Moon continues, and Neptune's influence heightens imagination and creativity. You may feel dreamy or unfocused in practical tasks, but this energy is perfect for artistic or spiritual pursuits. Music, writing, or meditation can open profound insights. Be cautious of illusions in relationships or money—clarity may be clouded. Lean into compassion, but don't sacrifice boundaries. Today, inspiration comes from subtle whispers, not loud declarations.

Gratitude Mantra

I am grateful for the creativity and compassion that flow through me, guiding me toward inspired action and deeper awareness.

Sagittarius
14 March 2026

The Moon enters fiery Aries, giving you a burst of energy and courage. Suddenly, your adventurous spirit feels reignited, and you're eager to take bold steps. Whether beginning a project, pursuing romance, or speaking your truth, today favours action over hesitation. Trust your instincts—they're sharp and daring. Be mindful of impatience, but don't suppress your fire. Momentum builds when you leap forward.

Gratitude Mantra

I am grateful for the fire within me that pushes me to take bold, inspired action.

Sagittarius
15 March 2026

With the Aries Moon energising you, passion and confidence run high. Your enthusiasm is contagious, drawing people toward your vision. This is a great day for leadership, creative projects, or simply enjoying life's adventures. Others may look to you for direction—step up with confidence. Balance is key, though; don't burn out by doing everything at once. Choose the projects that truly spark your joy.

Gratitude Mantra

I am grateful for my courage and the passion that lights my path and inspires others.

Sagittarius
16 March 2026

Mercury connects with Saturn, bringing a serious, thoughtful energy to conversations and planning. This is a day for making commitments or laying down practical structures for long-term success. Your adventurous mind may resist, but structure doesn't restrict you—it supports your freedom. Agreements made now have staying power. Don't avoid details; they'll anchor your big dreams.

Gratitude Mantra

I am grateful for the clarity and focus that allow me to turn ideas into lasting achievements.

Sagittarius
17 March 2026

The Moon in Taurus slows the pace, reminding you to enjoy life's simple pleasures. Nature, good food, music, or rest can restore your energy today. It's also a good time to tend to finances or practical matters. While it's not as exciting as adventure, grounding yourself provides the balance you need. Sagittarius, your fire burns brighter when paired with stability.

Gratitude Mantra

I am grateful for life's simple joys and the grounding energy that nourishes my spirit.

Sagittarius
18 March 2026

The Taurus Moon continues, encouraging patience and persistence. You may feel drawn to steady progress in career, health, or financial matters. This is a day to commit to your goals with determination, even if the rewards aren't immediate. Avoid stubbornness—flexibility will keep you moving forward. Trust that small, steady steps today will create lasting success tomorrow.

Gratitude Mantra

I am grateful for my determination and the patience to keep moving steadily toward my goals.

Sagittarius
19 March 2026

The Gemini Moon awakens your mind, sparking curiosity and a hunger for connection. Conversations flow easily, and you may find yourself bouncing between ideas, people, and projects. While this restless energy can scatter your focus, it also brings fresh inspiration and a sense of excitement. Use today to explore, learn, and ask questions. Your adventurous Sagittarian heart thrives when your mind is expanding, but remember to pace yourself—don't overcommit to every shiny distraction that appears.

Gratitude Mantra

I am grateful for my curious mind and the way new ideas expand my horizons.

Sagittarius
20 March 2026

The Sun enters Aries, igniting your fifth house of creativity, romance, and joy. This is a powerful cosmic boost for you, Sagittarius, as fiery Aries energy resonates with your adventurous nature. Today sparks passion, fun, and playful self-expression. You may feel inspired to create art, take a bold romantic step, or pursue a hobby that lights you up. Your confidence shines brightly, drawing others toward you. Let yourself fully embrace joy—it's fuel for your soul.

Gratitude Mantra

I am grateful for the joy, creativity, and passion that flow through me and uplift my spirit.

Sagittarius
21 March 2026

The Aries Moon continues to fire up your creativity, reminding you that life is best lived boldly. This is a day to pursue pleasure, adventure, and whatever makes your heart race. Your enthusiasm is infectious, and others are drawn to your spark. But be mindful not to spread yourself too thin or chase thrills without thought. Your greatest strength today lies in following your instincts with intention, turning passion into meaningful creation.

Gratitude Mantra

I am grateful for the courage to live boldly and the wisdom to channel my fire into purpose.

Sagittarius
22 March 2026

Mercury in Pisces squares Mars, which could create tension in communication. You may feel impatient or frustrated if others don't keep up with your pace or ideas. Sagittarius, you value honesty, but your bluntness could sting if not tempered with compassion. Think before speaking, especially in sensitive situations. Channel this fiery mental energy into problem-solving, writing, or planning rather than conflict. Clear words, spoken calmly, will move mountains more effectively than force.

Gratitude Mantra

I am grateful for the wisdom to pause, reflect, and speak with honesty and kindness.

Sagittarius
23 March 2026

The Moon shifts into Cancer, turning your focus to emotional security, family, and home. You may feel more sensitive or nostalgic, craving comfort and connection. This is a day for tending to relationships, sharing heartfelt conversations, or nurturing yourself. While you love adventure, Sagittarius, the universe reminds you that grounding in love and home gives strength to your explorations. Embrace tenderness—it deepens bonds and recharges your soul.

Gratitude Mantra

I am grateful for the love and emotional safety that nurture me and help me grow stronger.

Sagittarius
24 March 2026

The Cancer Moon continues, heightening your intuition and emotional awareness. Pay attention to dreams, gut instincts, and subtle signals from those around you. Your ability to sense what's unspoken is stronger today. This is a day for healing conversations, forgiveness, or simply offering support to loved ones. If emotions feel overwhelming, give yourself permission to rest and reflect. Compassion—both for yourself and others—will bring the clarity you seek.

Gratitude Mantra

I am grateful for my intuition and the compassion that guides me to deeper understanding.

Sagittarius
25 March 2026

A Full Moon in Libra lights up your house of friendships and community, bringing attention to the balance between independence and connection. Something within your social world may come to a climax—a project with friends, a group commitment, or even a relationship dynamic. Sagittarius, this is your chance to release what no longer aligns and embrace connections that uplift you. Honour your need for freedom while valuing the harmony of true companionship.

Gratitude Mantra

I am grateful for the friendships that uplift me and the freedom to honour my own path.

Sagittarius
26 March 2026

The Libra Moon still highlights your connections, encouraging collaboration, compromise, and balance. You may feel pulled between your own desires and the needs of others, but the lesson here is partnership. Sagittarius, you thrive in independence, yet today the cosmos reminds you of the strength found in teamwork. Whether through friendships, love, or professional ties, cooperation brings success. Don't view compromise as weakness—it's an art that strengthens bonds and creates harmony.

Gratitude Mantra

I am grateful for the balance and cooperation that enrich my relationships and open doors to greater success.

Sagittarius
27 March 2026

The Moon shifts into Scorpio, stirring deep emotions and sharpening your intuition. Today you may feel reflective, drawn to explore your inner world or uncover hidden truths in situations around you. While intensity may arise, don't shy away—it's through facing shadows that transformation occurs. Trust your instincts and allow vulnerability to guide you. Sagittarius, depth doesn't weaken your fire; it fuels your wisdom and creates profound growth.

Gratitude Mantra

I am grateful for the strength that comes from facing truth and embracing transformation.

Sagittarius
28 March 2026

With the Scorpio Moon intensifying your emotional world, you may feel drawn to tackle subjects you usually avoid. Conversations around intimacy, money, or trust may surface. While it could feel uncomfortable, there is healing available in honesty. Let your natural courage lead you through. Use today's energy for self-reflection, journaling, or heartfelt conversations that release old fears. What feels heavy now becomes the foundation for freedom later.

Gratitude Mantra

I am grateful for my courage to face the deep truths that set me free.

Sagittarius
29 March 2026

The Moon moves into Sagittarius, and your spirit feels reignited. Optimism, curiosity, and adventure return in full force. This is a day for travel, learning, or simply seeing life from a fresh perspective. Your energy inspires those around you, making this an excellent time to share your vision. Opportunities may arrive through conversations, new connections, or spontaneous invitations. Sagittarius, trust your instinct to leap—it's guiding you true.

Gratitude Mantra

I am grateful for the optimism and adventurous spirit that open doors to new experiences.

Sagittarius
30 March 2026

With the Moon still in your sign, your natural fire burns brightly. Today favours personal expression and independence—you'll want to follow your own path unapologetically. Your charisma attracts attention, and you may be asked to take the lead. Use your energy to push forward a personal project or simply celebrate who you are. Confidence is your ally, Sagittarius; let it light the way.

Gratitude Mantra

I am grateful for the confidence that empowers me to live authentically and boldly.

Sagittarius
31 March 2026

The Moon in Sagittarius forms supportive aspects, making this a day where opportunities align. You may feel as though luck is on your side—doors open, conversations flow, and inspiration is abundant. Don't waste this energy on hesitation. Say yes to invitations, try something new, and trust your instincts. The universe is encouraging movement forward. Sagittarius, you are at your best when embracing possibility.

Gratitude Mantra

I am grateful for the opportunities that flow toward me and the courage to embrace them.

April
2026

Sagittarius
1 April 2026

The Moon shifts into Capricorn, grounding your fiery energy. This is a day to focus on long-term goals, responsibilities, and achievements. While routine may feel less exciting than adventure, your future freedom depends on the foundations you build today. Discipline paired with your natural optimism creates unstoppable momentum. Take time to organise, plan, or commit to tasks that matter.

Gratitude Mantra

I am grateful for the discipline that supports my freedom and the focus that helps me achieve my dreams.

Sagittarius
2 April 2026

The Capricorn Moon continues, emphasising discipline, responsibility, and achievement. Today you may feel the weight of duties calling you, but don't see them as restrictions. Instead, recognise them as stepping stones toward your larger vision. Sagittarius, your fire thrives when supported by structure—it allows your adventurous spirit to soar without collapse. Tackle practical matters like career tasks, finances, or health routines. By putting in steady effort now, you create the freedom you crave later.

Gratitude Mantra

I am grateful for the steady effort that builds lasting foundations for my freedom and growth.

Sagittarius
3 April 2026

The Moon harmonises with Uranus, sparking sudden shifts in routine or career matters. You may find plans changing abruptly, but don't resist—it's the universe redirecting you toward a better path. Stay flexible and curious; surprises today can actually lead to breakthroughs. Your adventurous Sagittarian heart is wired for spontaneity, so embrace the unexpected. What feels like a detour may actually be divine timing guiding you toward opportunity.

Gratitude Mantra

I am grateful for the surprises that lead me to new opportunities and growth.

Sagittarius
4 April 2026

With the Moon moving into Aquarius, your focus shifts to friendships, groups, and community. Social connections carry extra importance today—you may find yourself inspired by the ideas or energy of others. Networking or teamwork could bring unexpected opportunities, so don't isolate. Share your vision; your optimism uplifts others. Collaboration is your strength now, reminding you that no dream is realised alone. Sagittarius, your role today is to bring fire to collective energy.

Gratitude Mantra

I am grateful for the connections and communities that inspire, support, and expand my dreams.

Sagittarius
5 April 2026

The Aquarius Moon highlights innovative thinking and originality. You may feel restless under routine, craving something new and exciting. Today is perfect for experimenting with different approaches or brainstorming unconventional solutions. Technology or progressive ideas may capture your attention, opening doors to fresh perspectives. Sagittarius, your gift is seeing beyond limits, and today the cosmos rewards outside-the-box vision. Don't hesitate to share your brilliance— it might spark transformation for yourself and others.

Gratitude Mantra

I am grateful for my innovative ideas and the courage to explore new possibilities.

Sagittarius
6 April 2026

Mercury aligns with Neptune, stirring intuition and imagination. Your mind feels dreamy and inspired, but it may be hard to focus on details. This is a day for creative writing, meditation, or spiritual practices rather than technical work. Be mindful of confusion in communication—clarify facts before making commitments. Your Sagittarian optimism blended with Neptune's vision can spark deep insights if you allow stillness.

Gratitude Mantra

I am grateful for the inspiration and intuition that guide me beyond logic into deeper truth.

Sagittarius
7 April 2026

The Moon in Pisces softens your energy, turning focus toward home, family, and emotional healing. You may feel called to retreat, rest, or spend time with loved ones. This is a day for nurturing both yourself and your closest bonds. Sagittarius, while adventure excites you, peace at home restores you. Don't overlook the power of comfort and connection—it strengthens your spirit for the journeys ahead.

Gratitude Mantra

I am grateful for the love and comfort that home and family bring to my life.

Sagittarius
8 April 2026

A New Moon Solar Eclipse in Aries sparks powerful new beginnings in creativity, romance, and self-expression. This is a cosmic reset, encouraging you to step boldly into passions that light you up. Sagittarius, this is your chance to embrace joy, fun, and personal freedom without apology. Plant seeds for projects, relationships, or adventures that reflect your true fire. Eclipses are catalysts for change—trust this new chapter.

Gratitude Mantra

I am grateful for new beginnings that align with my passions and ignite my spirit.

Sagittarius
09 April 2026

The Aries Moon continues to fuel passion, courage, and creativity in your life. You may feel a strong push to express yourself boldly, whether through art, romance, or adventure. Your energy is magnetic, and people are drawn to your enthusiasm. Be mindful not to burn out by chasing everything at once—choose the pursuits that truly excite your spirit. Sagittarius, your fire lights the way, but focus ensures your efforts leave a lasting mark.

Gratitude Mantra

I am grateful for the passion that drives me and the wisdom to channel it into meaningful pursuits.

Sagittarius
10 April 2026

With the Moon still in Aries, your adventurous spirit feels alive and restless. This is a day for taking action on something you've been hesitating over. Whether a creative project, a personal goal, or a heartfelt conversation, courage pays off now. Trust your instincts and take the leap—you'll be glad you did. Sagittarius, your daring nature shines brightest when you follow your truth without fear of judgement.

Gratitude Mantra

I am grateful for the courage to follow my instincts and step boldly into new experiences.

Sagittarius
11 April 2026

The Moon shifts into Taurus, slowing the pace and inviting you to ground yourself. After fiery, fast-moving days, you may feel relief in stability and routine. Focus on practical tasks—finances, health, or organisation. Nature and simple pleasures bring peace today, reminding you that slowing down is not losing momentum. Sagittarius, balance your fire with patience; both are needed for growth.

Gratitude Mantra

I am grateful for the peace and stability that grounding energy brings to my journey.

Sagittarius
12 April 2026

The Taurus Moon continues, asking you to value persistence and patience. You may feel drawn to review your goals, especially financial or career-related ones, with a practical lens. This is not about quick wins but long-term rewards. Your adventurous side may resist, but trust the process—foundations built now will sustain future freedom. Sagittarius, remember: true expansion is supported by steady roots.

Gratitude Mantra

I am grateful for my patience and the steady steps that carry me toward lasting success.

Sagittarius
13 April 2026

Venus aligns with Saturn, bringing seriousness to matters of love, money, and commitments. Relationships may feel tested today, asking for honesty, responsibility, and maturity. This is not a day for frivolity but for strengthening bonds. Financially, you may be prompted to take a more disciplined approach. Sagittarius, this cosmic energy reminds you that true freedom thrives when responsibilities are respected.

Gratitude Mantra

I am grateful for the discipline that strengthens my relationships and the wisdom that secures my future.

Sagittarius
14 April 2026

The Moon enters Gemini, activating curiosity, communication, and social connections. Your mind is buzzing with ideas, and conversations may open doors to exciting opportunities. While it's tempting to scatter your energy, choose a few priorities to pursue. Sagittarius, your natural charm shines today, making it easier to inspire others with your vision. Keep communication clear to avoid misunderstandings.

Gratitude Mantra

I am grateful for my curiosity and the opportunities that come from meaningful conversations and connections.

Sagittarius
15 April 2026

The Gemini Moon continues, amplifying your restlessness and need for variety. You may feel pulled in several directions at once—learning, socialising, or multitasking. While this energy brings inspiration, it can also scatter focus. Write down your ideas so you don't lose them, but don't feel pressured to chase them all today. Sagittarius, your gift is exploration; trust that the right path will become clear in time.

Gratitude Mantra

I am grateful for the inspiration and ideas that flow freely, guiding me toward new horizons.

Sagittarius
16 April 2026

The Gemini Moon squares Neptune, creating a fog around communication and plans. Misunderstandings may arise, and clarity may be hard to grasp. Avoid jumping to conclusions or making big decisions today—what you hear may not be the full story. Instead, use the dreamy energy for creativity, journaling, or meditation. Sagittarius, your optimism helps you see through confusion, but patience ensures you avoid unnecessary complications. Let clarity return before committing.

Gratitude Mantra

I am grateful for my ability to pause and trust that clarity always arrives at the right time.

Sagittarius
17 April 2026

The Moon shifts into Cancer, turning your attention toward home, family, and emotional comfort. You may feel sentimental or reflective, craving closeness with loved ones or simply a quiet space for yourself. This is a good day for nurturing bonds, cooking, or tending to your personal sanctuary. Sagittarius, while adventure calls to you, the cosmos reminds you that a strong home base fuels your journeys.

Gratitude Mantra

I am grateful for the comfort of home and the love that strengthens me for life's adventures.

Sagittarius
18 April 2026

The Cancer Moon continues, highlighting emotional needs and deepening your sensitivity. You may notice others turning to you for support or guidance, drawn by your warmth. While you love freedom, Sagittarius, your wisdom also shines in moments of compassion and care. Balance your needs with the needs of others—giving too much could drain you. Today is about creating emotional harmony for yourself and those around you.

Gratitude Mantra

I am grateful for my compassion and the healing energy it brings to myself and others.

Sagittarius
19 April 2026

The Sun enters Taurus, shifting focus toward stability, work, and the physical world. Over the next month, your energy may be drawn to finances, routines, and long-term planning. Today is a good time to set realistic goals and commit to steady action. Sagittarius, while you thrive on excitement, grounding yourself in practical matters ensures your fire continues to burn brightly. Treat stability as your ally.

Gratitude Mantra

I am grateful for the stability and structure that support my dreams and adventures.

Sagittarius
20 April 2026

With the Cancer Moon opposing Pluto, emotions may intensify. Power struggles or hidden truths could surface in relationships or family matters. While intensity can feel uncomfortable, facing it honestly leads to transformation. Sagittarius, your blunt honesty can help cut through drama, but soften it with empathy. This is a day for emotional release—don't suppress feelings. What is acknowledged now becomes a stepping stone toward growth and freedom.

Gratitude Mantra

I am grateful for the strength to face emotional truths and the wisdom to grow from them.

Sagittarius
21 April 2026

The Moon enters Leo, rekindling your fire and sense of adventure. Creativity, playfulness, and self-expression take the spotlight. You may feel more confident, eager to take risks or share your ideas with the world. This is a wonderful day to reconnect with your passions, enjoy romance, or simply have fun. Sagittarius, your enthusiasm uplifts others—shine brightly and unapologetically.

Gratitude Mantra

I am grateful for my confidence and the joy that comes from expressing my true self.

Sagittarius
22 April 2026

The Leo Moon continues, highlighting your leadership qualities. Others look to you for direction, and your bold energy can inspire the group. This is a perfect time for creative collaboration, socialising, or stepping into a role where your vision matters. Sagittarius, be mindful not to dominate—true leadership uplifts and empowers others. Today, your courage and enthusiasm can light the way for many.

Gratitude Mantra

I am grateful for the courage to lead with passion and the wisdom to inspire others positively.

Sagittarius
23 April 2026

The Leo Moon continues to amplify creativity, romance, and self-expression. Today you may feel inspired to step into the spotlight, whether through work, love, or creative pursuits. Your charisma shines brightly, attracting opportunities and admiration. Be mindful not to seek validation solely from others—confidence grows stronger when it comes from within. Sagittarius, use this energy to celebrate your unique gifts and share them with the world. Your joy is contagious when expressed authentically.

Gratitude Mantra

I am grateful for my unique light and the confidence to share it with the world.

Sagittarius
24 April 2026

The Moon shifts into Virgo, turning your focus toward work, routines, and organisation. Details may demand attention today, and though you prefer the big picture, tackling the small stuff brings clarity. This is an excellent time to declutter, refine plans, or focus on health habits. Sagittarius, remember that adventure thrives when life is well-ordered. By tending to the details now, you free space for future expansion.

Gratitude Mantra

I am grateful for the clarity and structure that come from tending to life's details with care.

Sagittarius
25 April 2026

With the Virgo Moon highlighting routines, you may feel pulled toward productivity and self-improvement. While perfectionism can creep in, avoid being overly critical of yourself or others. Progress, not perfection, is the goal. Use this energy to organise projects or improve daily habits. Sagittarius, your fire thrives when paired with practical grounding. Today, small adjustments have the power to transform your bigger journey over time.

Gratitude Mantra

I am grateful for progress made through small, steady steps that create lasting change.

Sagittarius
26 April 2026

The Virgo Moon harmonises with Pluto, helping you dig deeper into tasks and transform how you approach work and health. You may uncover a better system, habit, or perspective that makes life easier. This is a day for serious focus but also deep breakthroughs. Sagittarius, your gift is big vision, and today you can blend that with practical action for powerful results.

Gratitude Mantra

I am grateful for the breakthroughs that come when vision meets focus and persistence.

Sagittarius
27 April 2026

The Moon enters Libra, shifting attention toward partnerships, harmony, and balance. Relationships of all kinds take centre stage—romantic, friendship, or professional. Compromise and cooperation are favoured today, but don't lose sight of your own needs. Sagittarius, you thrive in freedom, yet true growth comes when independence meets connection. Seek harmony without sacrificing authenticity, and you'll strengthen bonds that matter most.

Gratitude Mantra

I am grateful for the balance between independence and connection that keeps my relationships strong.

Sagittarius
28 April 2026

The Libra Moon continues, encouraging diplomacy, fairness, and collaboration. You may find yourself mediating conflicts, offering support, or working to restore harmony. Your natural honesty combined with tact can resolve issues smoothly. This is also a good day for partnerships, contracts, or creative collaborations. Sagittarius, your wisdom shines brightest when you blend truth with kindness —today is your chance to do just that.

Gratitude Mantra

I am grateful for the harmony and cooperation that create peace in my relationships.

Sagittarius
29 April 2026

The Moon in Libra opposes Chiron, highlighting healing in relationships. Old wounds may resurface, but they do so to be released, not relived. Honest conversations can help you and others move forward. Sagittarius, while you prefer to look ahead, healing requires pausing to acknowledge the past. Use today's energy for forgiveness, understanding, and emotional release—it lightens your spirit for the road ahead.

Gratitude Mantra

I am grateful for the healing that comes from forgiveness and honesty in relationships.

Sagittarius
30 April 2026

The Moon shifts into Scorpio, bringing intensity, reflection, and emotional depth. You may feel drawn to explore your inner world, question old patterns, or dive into topics that have long fascinated you. Secrets may come to light, and you'll need to decide how to handle them—with honesty and wisdom. Relationships could feel magnetic yet intense, as deeper layers emerge. Sagittarius, while you thrive on freedom, don't overlook the power of transformation. Facing truths now helps you step into greater authenticity and personal strength.

Gratitude Mantra

I am grateful for the strength to face deep truths and the wisdom to transform challenges into growth.

May 2026

Sagittarius
1 May 2026

The Scorpio Moon continues, urging you to embrace depth and emotional honesty. Today may feel heavier than usual, but it's an opportunity for healing and release. If you've been avoiding difficult conversations, the cosmos encourages you to face them with courage. Your instincts are sharp now—trust them when navigating tricky situations. Sagittarius, transformation often begins in uncomfortable places, yet it ultimately frees your spirit to soar. Embrace what surfaces today as part of your growth.

Gratitude Mantra

I am grateful for my courage to face challenges honestly and the freedom that comes from transformation.

Sagittarius
2 May 2026

The Moon enters Sagittarius, lifting your spirit and reigniting your adventurous fire. Optimism, enthusiasm, and curiosity flow easily today, making it perfect for travel, learning, or trying something new. Your natural charisma shines, drawing people to you and opening doors to fresh opportunities. This is a day for exploration in every sense—physical, intellectual, or spiritual. Sagittarius, follow your instincts boldly; the universe supports your leaps of faith and rewards your courage.

Gratitude Mantra

I am grateful for my adventurous nature and the opportunities it brings to expand my horizons.

Sagittarius
3 May 2026

With the Moon still in your sign, confidence and enthusiasm peak. You may feel restless if tied down, craving freedom and new experiences. This is the time to pursue personal goals, assert your independence, and embrace activities that bring joy. Your optimism inspires others, but be mindful not to overwhelm them with your pace. Sagittarius, your strength today lies in living authentically, boldly, and unapologetically. Shine your light brightly—others will follow your lead.

Gratitude Mantra

I am grateful for my confidence and the freedom to live boldly and authentically.

Sagittarius
4 May 2026

The Moon in Sagittarius forms supportive aspects, making this a day where luck and opportunity align. Doors may open in unexpected ways, whether through travel, education, or chance encounters. Your adventurous spirit is rewarded, but stay mindful of overcommitment. Focus on what truly excites you, and say yes to opportunities that align with your bigger vision. Sagittarius, the universe is nudging you forward—embrace the journey with trust and excitement.

Gratitude Mantra

I am grateful for the opportunities that flow to me and the courage to embrace them wholeheartedly.

Sagittarius
5 May 2026

The Moon moves into Capricorn, bringing focus, responsibility, and structure. After fiery days of exploration, today asks you to ground your energy and commit to long-term goals. This is an excellent time to review finances, career plans, or health routines. Sagittarius, while discipline isn't always your favourite, it supports your freedom by creating security. Think of today as building the scaffolding for the adventures you dream of tomorrow.

Gratitude Mantra

I am grateful for the discipline and focus that help me create a strong foundation for future freedom.

Sagittarius
6 May 2026

The Capricorn Moon continues, highlighting ambition, career, and practical matters. You may be called to prove your reliability, step into leadership, or demonstrate responsibility. Though you prefer spontaneity, steady effort is needed today. Your determination and optimism can help you handle any challenge. Take pride in what you've achieved so far, but stay committed to the path ahead. Sagittarius, success is built brick by brick—each step matters more than you realise.

Gratitude Mantra

I am grateful for the persistence and determination that carry me closer to my long-term goals.

Sagittarius
07 May 2026

The Moon in Capricorn aligns with Uranus, bringing sudden shifts to your daily rhythm. Plans may change unexpectedly, or new responsibilities may appear out of nowhere. Instead of resisting, embrace the shake-up—Sagittarius, you thrive in spontaneity, and this twist could lead to exciting opportunities. Use your adventurous spirit to adapt quickly, and don't be afraid to try unconventional approaches. What looks disruptive at first may be a cosmic nudge toward something better. Trust the redirection—it's part of your greater journey.

Gratitude Mantra

I am grateful for my adaptability and the way surprises often guide me toward new opportunities.

Sagittarius
08 May 2026

The Moon enters Aquarius, turning your focus toward friendships, social groups, and community connections. You may feel inspired by shared ideas or collaborative projects, and your unique perspective can spark meaningful conversations. Technology, innovation, or networking may play a role in today's opportunities. Sagittarius, your role is to contribute your fire and vision to the group while also remaining open to learning from others. Teamwork is favoured, and your natural optimism uplifts everyone involved.

Gratitude Mantra

I am grateful for the friendships and collaborations that inspire me and expand my world.

Sagittarius
09 May 2026

With the Aquarius Moon highlighting innovation, you're encouraged to think outside the box. Today, new solutions may arise through brainstorming or unexpected inspiration. Be open to unconventional ideas and trust that fresh approaches can solve long-standing issues. Social interactions bring insight, and you may meet someone whose perspective broadens your own. Sagittarius, your adventurous spirit thrives when you step outside the ordinary—today, embrace the extraordinary and allow it to reshape your vision.

Gratitude Mantra

I am grateful for innovative ideas and the inspiration that comes from seeing life from new perspectives.

Sagittarius
10 May 2026

The Aquarius Moon forms supportive aspects, making this an excellent day for teamwork, learning, and visionary pursuits. Big-picture thinking comes naturally now, and your optimism helps groups overcome challenges. You may feel drawn to causes bigger than yourself, seeking ways to contribute to collective progress. Sagittarius, your wisdom and enthusiasm inspire others to believe in what's possible. Trust that your voice carries weight—it can spark real change when used with intention and purpose.

Gratitude Mantra

I am grateful for my ability to inspire and uplift others through vision and enthusiasm.

Sagittarius
11 May 2026

The Moon shifts into Pisces, drawing your attention to home, emotions, and spiritual reflection. You may feel more sensitive today, craving peace and comfort. This is a perfect time to retreat, meditate, or spend time with loved ones. Creativity also flows strongly—art, music, or writing could bring emotional release. Sagittarius, while your heart often longs for adventure, today the cosmos reminds you of the importance of rest and inner healing.

Gratitude Mantra

I am grateful for the peace and healing that come from nurturing my inner world and home.

Sagittarius
12 May 2026

The Pisces Moon continues, bringing heightened intuition and imagination. You may sense unspoken feelings in others or notice synchronicities guiding your path. This is a day for listening inward rather than pushing forward. While practical tasks may feel draining, creative or spiritual activities energise you. Sagittarius, let go of the need for logic—allow intuition to show you the way forward. The answers you seek are already within you.

Gratitude Mantra

I am grateful for my intuition and the guidance it provides in quiet, subtle ways.

Sagittarius
13 May 2026

The Pisces Moon aligns with Jupiter, your ruling planet, amplifying optimism, compassion, and creativity. Opportunities may flow easily today, especially in areas of spirituality, relationships, or personal growth. You may feel inspired to help others, share your wisdom, or embrace a new creative pursuit. Your generosity and open heart attract blessings now. Sagittarius, this is a reminder that when you follow joy and compassion, abundance naturally follows. Embrace the magic of the day.

Gratitude Mantra

I am grateful for the joy and abundance that flow when I live with compassion and generosity.

Sagittarius
14 May 2026

The Moon moves into Aries, reigniting your adventurous spirit and sparking courage. Today you feel restless, eager to take action, and unwilling to settle for routine. This fiery energy is excellent for starting new projects, taking risks, or expressing your passions openly. You may feel more competitive or determined to prove yourself, but remember to channel this drive constructively. Sagittarius, trust your instincts—this is a day for bold moves, but balance them with wisdom to avoid reckless leaps.

Gratitude Mantra

I am grateful for my courage to take bold steps and the wisdom to guide my fire with purpose.

Sagittarius
15 May 2026

The Aries Moon continues, boosting your confidence and passion. Your enthusiasm is infectious, drawing others to your energy and vision. This is a powerful day for leadership and self-expression—you may be called to take charge or inspire others. Use this influence to push forward personal goals or pursue creative passions. Be mindful of impatience or impulsive actions, but don't dim your fire. Sagittarius, your bravery inspires growth both within yourself and those around you.

Gratitude Mantra

I am grateful for my confidence and the passion that fuels my journey and uplifts others.

Sagittarius
16 May 2026

With the Aries Moon forming tense aspects, you may feel more impatient than usual. Frustrations could arise if progress feels slow or if others don't match your pace. Instead of reacting impulsively, pause and breathe—this is a chance to practice patience while still channelling your drive. Physical activity helps burn off excess energy, so consider exercise, movement, or outdoor adventure. Sagittarius, this test of restraint helps you sharpen your focus and channel your fire wisely.

Gratitude Mantra

I am grateful for my ability to turn restlessness into focused action and growth.

Sagittarius
17 May 2026

The Moon shifts into Taurus, encouraging stability, grounding, and appreciation of life's simple pleasures. After fiery energy, today feels calmer and more practical. Focus on building routines, tending to finances, or grounding yourself in nature. While you thrive on excitement, Sagittarius, this slower pace reminds you that stability is what sustains freedom. Use today to commit to steady progress—your adventurous future depends on the foundations you create now.

Gratitude Mantra

I am grateful for the grounding energy that steadies my spirit and supports my bigger dreams.

Sagittarius
18 May 2026

The Taurus Moon continues, highlighting persistence and patience. Progress may feel slow, but this energy helps you build lasting results. Focus on health habits, finances, or career steps that require consistency. While your fiery side craves immediate results, today teaches the power of slow and steady effort. Sagittarius, trust that each small action lays groundwork for greater adventures ahead. This is not a day for rushing—it's for building.

Gratitude Mantra

I am grateful for my patience and the steady effort that leads me toward lasting success.

Sagittarius
19 May 2026

The Taurus Moon aligns with Pluto, deepening your focus and determination. Today you may uncover a powerful new approach to your goals or finally release a limiting belief. Transformation is available if you're willing to dig deep and commit. Sagittarius, while you prefer lightness, don't shy from intensity—it brings breakthroughs. Whether financial, personal, or emotional, what you transform today paves the way for long-term growth and freedom.

Gratitude Mantra

I am grateful for the strength to embrace transformation and the clarity it brings to my path.

Sagittarius
20 May 2026

The Sun enters Gemini, bringing fresh energy to communication, learning, and relationships. Over the coming month, your focus turns to curiosity, connection, and mental exploration. Today, conversations spark inspiration and opportunities, while your words carry weight. Sagittarius, you thrive when exchanging ideas, teaching, or learning new things. This is your season to expand through knowledge and connection—embrace it with openness and enthusiasm. The universe wants you to explore in every sense.

Gratitude Mantra

I am grateful for the curiosity and connections that expand my mind and enrich my journey.

Sagittarius
21 May 2026

The Gemini Moon joins the Sun, amplifying your need for communication, learning, and connection. This is a day for conversations that spark ideas, new collaborations, and social interactions that energise you. Your natural curiosity thrives now, and you may find yourself exploring multiple interests at once. Sagittarius, while variety excites you, don't scatter your energy too thin. Choose a few paths that align with your vision and commit. Inspiration flows when you remain both open and focused.

Gratitude Mantra

I am grateful for the connections and ideas that inspire me and expand my horizons.

Sagittarius
22 May 2026

The Gemini Moon continues, making today lively, social, and thought-provoking. You may feel restless, eager to learn, and open to change. Conversations could lead to surprising opportunities or new perspectives. Be mindful of overthinking or speaking impulsively—choose your words carefully, as they carry influence. Sagittarius, your wisdom blends beautifully with your curiosity now, helping you share knowledge while learning from others. Let today's energy fuel both fun and growth.

Gratitude Mantra

I am grateful for my curiosity and the wisdom that comes from learning through meaningful conversations.

Sagittarius
23 May 2026

The Moon moves into Cancer, shifting focus toward emotions, family, and security. You may crave comfort or feel nostalgic, reflecting on where you come from and how it shapes your journey. Relationships may feel more sensitive today, and compassion is needed. Sagittarius, while you thrive on freedom, home and emotional grounding give you strength for adventure. Honour your feelings and nurture those closest to you—you'll feel lighter and more supported as a result.

Gratitude Mantra

I am grateful for the emotional grounding that home and family bring to my life.

Sagittarius
24 May 2026

The Cancer Moon continues, highlighting intuition, compassion, and the need for emotional balance. You may feel more attuned to others' needs, but avoid taking on too much of their energy. Create space for self-care alongside nurturing others. Sagittarius, your wisdom shines when you blend honesty with kindness—offer support without losing yourself in the process. Dreams or intuitive nudges may bring guidance now. Trust the messages from your heart and the universe.

Gratitude Mantra

I am grateful for my intuition and the compassion that guides me in helping others without losing myself.

Sagittarius
25 May 2026

A Full Moon in Sagittarius lights up your sign, bringing a powerful climax to personal goals and self-expression. This is a time of release and realisation—something you've been working toward may reach fulfilment, or you may feel called to let go of limiting patterns. Your confidence, optimism, and adventurous nature are highlighted. Sagittarius, embrace this spotlight with honesty and courage. Celebrate your progress, release what holds you back, and step boldly into the next chapter.

Gratitude Mantra

I am grateful for the light that shines on my growth and the courage to embrace new beginnings.

Sagittarius
26 May 2026

With the Full Moon energy still strong, you may feel heightened emotions and clarity about your path forward. This is an excellent day for reflection, journaling, or setting new intentions. Your fiery nature may push you to act immediately, but pause first—clarity comes when you allow yourself to process. Sagittarius, you're stepping into greater alignment with your authentic self. Trust the wisdom gained through reflection and use it to fuel purposeful action.

Gratitude Mantra

I am grateful for the clarity that comes from reflection and the courage to align with my true path.

Sagittarius
27 May 2026

The Moon enters Capricorn, grounding the fiery energy of the Full Moon. Today is about putting practical steps behind the big visions you've set. Focus on career, responsibilities, or building structure around your goals. While you prefer freedom, Sagittarius, structure supports your long-term adventures. Use this day to plan carefully, handle details, and commit to consistent effort. Your determination, paired with optimism, makes you unstoppable now. Lay down the bricks for your future freedom.

Gratitude Mantra

I am grateful for the structure and discipline that strengthen my path and fuel my freedom.

Sagittarius
28 May 2026

The Capricorn Moon continues, emphasising focus, responsibility, and perseverance. You may feel the push to work hard or prove yourself in professional matters. This is a day to take steady, deliberate steps rather than seeking shortcuts. Career goals, financial planning, or even health routines benefit from your attention now. Sagittarius, while discipline may not feel as exciting as adventure, it supports your long-term freedom. Trust that the structures you build today will sustain the dreams you chase tomorrow. Consistency is your ally.

Gratitude Mantra

I am grateful for the steady effort that builds a secure foundation for my future adventures.

Sagittarius
29 May 2026

The Capricorn Moon harmonises with Uranus, bringing surprising insights or changes in career and daily routines. Plans may shift suddenly, opening unexpected opportunities. While disruptions may feel inconvenient, they're guiding you toward growth. Stay adaptable and open to fresh approaches—you may find a better way of doing things than you imagined. Sagittarius, your gift is flexibility, and today it helps you thrive. Trust that even detours are part of the greater map of your destiny.

Gratitude Mantra

I am grateful for my adaptability and the opportunities that come through unexpected changes.

Sagittarius
30 May 2026

The Moon enters Aquarius, turning your focus toward friendships, groups, and collaboration. This is a day where teamwork and shared vision bring exciting breakthroughs. Conversations with friends may spark inspiration or reveal opportunities you hadn't considered. Sagittarius, your adventurous mind thrives when bouncing ideas with others, and today you'll find energy flows best in community. Be willing to listen as much as you speak—collective wisdom will expand your perspective.

Gratitude Mantra

I am grateful for the inspiration and opportunities that come through shared ideas and connections.

Sagittarius
31 May 2026

With the Aquarius Moon energising your social zone, you may feel restless under routine and eager to connect with like-minded souls. Community, friendships, or group projects bring fulfilment today. You may even find yourself drawn to humanitarian or progressive causes that resonate with your values. Sagittarius, your optimism inspires others, and when you bring your energy to a group, it multiplies. Seek collaboration, but don't lose sight of your individuality—it's your spark that makes the difference.

Gratitude Mantra

I am grateful for the communities that inspire me and the individuality that keeps my fire unique.

June
2026

Sagittarius
1 June 2026

The Moon in Aquarius aligns with Jupiter, your ruling planet, amplifying optimism, social charm, and inspiration. This is one of those rare days where things seem to fall into place effortlessly. Friendships feel warm, opportunities may arise through networking, and your confidence shines. Sagittarius, your words and presence carry extra influence today—use them to uplift others and share your vision. The more joy you radiate, the more abundance flows toward you.

Gratitude Mantra

I am grateful for the joy and abundance that flow when I share my light with others.

Sagittarius
2 June 2026

The Moon moves into Pisces, shifting focus to home, emotions, and intuition. After lively days, you may crave peace and solitude. This is a good day to rest, reflect, or reconnect with loved ones. Creativity also flows strongly now, so writing, art, or music can bring healing. Sagittarius, while your adventurous side seeks constant movement, the cosmos reminds you that quiet moments of reflection bring the deepest wisdom. Honour stillness—it strengthens you.

Gratitude Mantra

I am grateful for the peace and wisdom that arise in still, quiet moments.

Sagittarius
3 June 2026

The Pisces Moon continues, deepening sensitivity and compassion. You may feel more connected to others' emotions, and your empathy could be a guiding force. Be mindful not to absorb negativity—set gentle boundaries while still offering support. Spiritual practices, dreams, or meditation may reveal guidance now. Sagittarius, your adventurous heart also thrives in exploration of the unseen and mystical—lean into that today. Answers may come in subtle, unexpected ways.

Gratitude Mantra

I am grateful for my compassion and the intuitive guidance that helps me support others while honouring myself.

Sagittarius
04 June 2026

A New Moon in Gemini highlights your house of partnerships, communication, and collaboration. This is a powerful reset for relationships, offering you the chance to begin fresh cycles in love, friendships, or professional alliances. Honest conversations pave the way for greater understanding, and new agreements may be formed. Sagittarius, this lunation invites you to balance your independence with meaningful connections. Plant seeds for relationships that reflect your truth. This is the start of a chapter where collaboration and communication will help you grow beyond what you could achieve alone.

Gratitude Mantra

I am grateful for the new beginnings in relationships and the connections that help me grow.

Sagittarius
05 June 2026

The Gemini Moon continues to energise your communication zone, sparking conversations, learning, and social activity. You may feel pulled in many directions, with invitations, ideas, or opportunities coming at you all at once. While your enthusiasm is infectious, be mindful of overextending yourself. Sagittarius, your adventurous nature loves variety, but today's challenge is focus. Choose what truly excites your spirit and let go of the rest. Clear intentions now ensure your energy supports growth rather than scattering.

Gratitude Mantra

I am grateful for the clarity to focus my energy on what truly excites and uplifts me.

Sagittarius
06 June 2026

The Moon moves into Cancer, turning your attention to emotional needs, home life, and security. You may feel more reflective and sensitive, craving connection with loved ones or time to nurture yourself. Old feelings may resurface, giving you a chance to heal or release them. Sagittarius, while you thrive on movement and adventure, today's lesson is that true strength comes from emotional grounding. Honour your need for comfort—it will refuel you for the road ahead.

Gratitude Mantra

I am grateful for the love and comfort that restore my energy and strengthen my spirit.

Sagittarius
7 June 2026

The Cancer Moon continues, heightening intuition and emotional awareness. You may feel extra attuned to others' moods, making compassion and patience important today. This is an ideal time for heartfelt conversations, creative expression, or simply resting in a safe, nurturing space. Sagittarius, your wisdom shines when you balance honesty with empathy —today, it's not about big adventures, but small, meaningful connections that remind you of what truly matters.

Gratitude Mantra

I am grateful for my intuition and the heartfelt connections that deepen my understanding of others.

Sagittarius
8 June 2026

The Moon in Leo reignites your fire, bringing passion, creativity, and confidence. After days of introspection, you're ready to shine again. This is a day to express yourself boldly, take risks, or pursue joy unapologetically. Romance and creativity are highlighted, and your magnetic energy draws people to you. Sagittarius, your natural spark inspires others —today is about celebrating your uniqueness and embracing life with enthusiasm. Let your fire light the way for others.

Gratitude Mantra

I am grateful for my confidence and the fire that inspires joy in myself and others.

Sagittarius
9 June 2026

The Leo Moon continues, making this a day for bold action and playful confidence. Opportunities to lead, inspire, or create are strong now. Your charisma is magnetic, and people may look to you for direction. While your fiery enthusiasm is a gift, balance it with humility—leadership thrives when it empowers others. Sagittarius, your courage shines brightest when it sparks courage in those around you. Step forward with authenticity and joy.

Gratitude Mantra

I am grateful for the courage to lead with authenticity and the joy it brings to others.

Sagittarius
10 June 2026

The Moon in Leo forms supportive aspects, amplifying opportunities for growth, creativity, and fun. This is a day where your adventurous spirit feels completely alive. Social connections, creative pursuits, or bold personal projects flourish now. You may feel unstoppable, ready to take risks that once felt daunting. Sagittarius, your fiery optimism is your greatest strength—when you trust your instincts, magic unfolds. Share your light freely; it's contagious and uplifting for everyone around you.

Gratitude Mantra

I am grateful for the optimism and creativity that fuel my journey and inspire others.

Sagittarius
11 June 2026

The Moon shifts into Virgo, directing your energy toward work, routines, and responsibilities. After fiery Leo days, this grounding energy may feel slower, but it helps you organise your goals. Focus on practical tasks, health, or financial matters that need attention. Don't see this as mundane, Sagittarius—it's the universe reminding you that details matter. Small, steady steps now support the big adventures you dream of later. Balance inspiration with discipline, and you'll build something lasting.

Gratitude Mantra

I am grateful for the grounding energy that helps me stay focused and build a strong foundation.

Sagittarius
12 June 2026

The Virgo Moon continues, encouraging productivity, organisation, and problem-solving. You may feel called to refine your routines or fix things that have been left unfinished. While you usually thrive on big ideas, today is about details and discipline. Sagittarius, your adventurous fire sometimes resists structure, but this energy teaches you that freedom is supported by stability. Honour your responsibilities now—they'll give you the space to pursue your passions later with ease.

Gratitude Mantra

I am grateful for the clarity and focus that come from tending to details with care.

Sagittarius
13 June 2026

The Moon in Virgo harmonises with Pluto, helping you dig deep into your goals and transform habits that no longer serve you. This is a powerful day for self-improvement, whether through health, career, or personal growth. You may uncover hidden strengths or realise what's been holding you back. Sagittarius, transformation requires honesty—face the truth, and you'll find your fire burning brighter than before. Let discipline and vision merge into powerful momentum.

Gratitude Mantra

I am grateful for the strength to transform habits and the clarity to step into my power.

Sagittarius
14 June 2026

The Moon shifts into Libra, turning focus toward partnerships, balance, and connection. Relationships of all kinds may feel highlighted, and you're asked to consider both your needs and the needs of others. Compromise is key today, but not at the cost of your authenticity. Sagittarius, you thrive on independence, but meaningful connections also nourish you. This is a day for harmony, fairness, and building bridges through empathy and truth.

Gratitude Mantra

I am grateful for the balance between independence and connection that strengthens my relationships.

Sagittarius
15 June 2026

The Libra Moon continues, emphasising diplomacy and cooperation. You may find yourself mediating conflicts, supporting friends, or working in collaboration toward shared goals. Your honesty and optimism make you a natural peacemaker, Sagittarius, but remember that balance means honouring your truth as well. Partnerships flourish when honesty and kindness meet. Be open to different perspectives—they may expand your vision in unexpected ways. Today, harmony is both your gift and your responsibility.

Gratitude Mantra

I am grateful for the harmony and cooperation that bring peace and growth into my relationships.

Sagittarius
16 June 2026

The Libra Moon opposes Chiron, bringing opportunities for healing in relationships. Old wounds may resurface, asking for compassion and forgiveness. While it may feel uncomfortable, this is a chance to release lingering pain and strengthen connections. Sagittarius, you prefer to look forward, but healing requires looking back with honesty. Embrace vulnerability—it's the key to growth. Today's energy helps you turn pain into wisdom and rebuild trust where it's needed.

Gratitude Mantra

I am grateful for the healing that comes from compassion, honesty, and forgiveness.

Sagittarius
17 June 2026

The Moon moves into Scorpio, intensifying emotions and sharpening intuition. You may feel more reflective, drawn to uncover hidden truths in yourself or others. This is a day for depth, not surface-level interactions. Sagittarius, while your nature seeks freedom and lightness, transformation comes through depth and honesty. Don't shy away from what feels intense—it has lessons to teach. Use this energy for healing, journaling, or meaningful conversations that spark growth.

Gratitude Mantra

I am grateful for my courage to face depth and the transformation it brings.

Sagittarius
18 June 2026

The Scorpio Moon continues, bringing intensity, passion, and emotional depth. You may feel pulled toward uncovering truths, healing wounds, or facing subjects you'd usually avoid. While this energy can feel heavy, it's transformative, helping you release what no longer serves you. Sagittarius, your adventurous spirit prefers lightness, but depth brings wisdom you can't find elsewhere. Embrace vulnerability, honesty, and transformation—they strengthen your fire for the journey ahead. Use today for journaling, deep conversations, or inner reflection.

Gratitude Mantra

I am grateful for the courage to face deep emotions and the wisdom that grows from transformation.

Sagittarius
19 June 2026

The Scorpio Moon harmonises with Neptune, heightening your intuition and creative imagination. Dreams, synchronicities, and gut feelings may offer insight today. You may feel drawn to spiritual practices, art, or time spent in quiet reflection. While practical matters may feel overwhelming, your inner compass points you in the right direction. Sagittarius, you thrive when trusting your instincts, and today your intuition is especially sharp—follow it. Inspiration and healing are close at hand if you remain open.

Gratitude Mantra

I am grateful for my intuition and the guidance it brings through subtle signs and inner knowing.

Sagittarius
20 June 2026

The Moon moves into Sagittarius, lifting your energy and reigniting your optimism. After days of emotional heaviness, your adventurous spirit is ready to soar again. This is a day for travel, exploration, or trying something bold and new. Your confidence shines, and people are drawn to your enthusiasm. Opportunities may appear through chance encounters or spontaneous decisions. Sagittarius, when you trust your instincts and leap, the universe meets you halfway.

Gratitude Mantra

I am grateful for my adventurous spirit and the confidence to embrace new horizons with joy.

Sagittarius
21 June 2026

A Full Moon in Sagittarius illuminates your sign, bringing personal growth, realisations, and a sense of culmination. Something you've been working toward may come to fruition, or you may finally release limiting beliefs that held you back. This is a powerful moment of clarity—your truth is highlighted, and it's time to step fully into your authenticity. Sagittarius, celebrate your progress, honour your journey, and let go of what no longer aligns with who you are becoming.

Gratitude Mantra

I am grateful for the clarity and courage to live in alignment with my authentic self.

Sagittarius
22 June 2026

With the Full Moon energy still strong, emotions may feel heightened, and clarity about your path forward continues to unfold. This is a day for integration—reflect on recent breakthroughs and set intentions for the next chapter. Sagittarius, your fiery optimism propels you forward, but don't rush. Pause, process, and honour the lessons. True growth comes when you align passion with purpose. Use today to recalibrate, then move forward with renewed energy and wisdom.

Gratitude Mantra

I am grateful for the clarity and wisdom that help me align passion with purpose.

Sagittarius
23 June 2026

The Moon shifts into Capricorn, grounding your fiery energy. After the high of the Full Moon, today asks for focus, responsibility, and practical steps. Work, finances, or long-term planning benefit from your attention now. While you prefer freedom, Sagittarius, structure sustains your adventurous lifestyle. Think of today as building the scaffolding for future adventures. Balance discipline with optimism, and you'll feel both secure and inspired. Small, steady steps matter most now.

Gratitude Mantra

I am grateful for the balance of discipline and optimism that builds my future freedom.

Sagittarius
24 June 2026

The Capricorn Moon continues, emphasising ambition and perseverance. You may be called to prove your reliability, take on responsibility, or show leadership in your work or community. While this energy can feel demanding, it's also empowering—Sagittarius, you're more capable than you think. By committing to steady effort, you'll see long-term rewards. Remember, success isn't built in leaps but in consistent steps. Trust yourself, and know your adventurous fire is stronger when supported by stability.

Gratitude Mantra

I am grateful for the determination and perseverance that carry me closer to lasting success.

Sagittarius
25 June 2026

The Capricorn Moon forms supportive aspects, encouraging steady effort and focus. This is a day to get serious about long-term goals, whether financial, career, or personal. While you prefer freedom, Sagittarius, the cosmos reminds you that discipline creates the foundation for adventure. A practical conversation may bring clarity or an authority figure could recognise your efforts. Don't underestimate the power of consistent steps—they are paving the way for your dreams. Success today comes not from speed but from persistence and patience.

Gratitude Mantra

I am grateful for the steady progress that builds a secure and lasting foundation for my dreams.

Sagittarius
26 June 2026

The Moon enters Aquarius, shifting your focus toward friendships, groups, and shared visions. You may feel inspired by conversations with like-minded people or drawn to collaborate on a project. Technology, innovation, or community activities may play an important role now. Sagittarius, your adventurous spirit thrives when surrounded by those who expand your worldview. Be open to fresh perspectives—they may spark breakthroughs. Today is about connection, collaboration, and exploring how your fire contributes to a bigger picture.

Gratitude Mantra

I am grateful for the connections and collaborations that expand my vision and enrich my journey.

Sagittarius
27 June 2026

The Aquarius Moon continues, amplifying your originality and desire for freedom. You may feel restless with routine and crave excitement, new ideas, or unconventional experiences. Friendships and social circles provide inspiration now, and you may encounter someone who challenges your perspective in a positive way. Sagittarius, your gift is exploring beyond limits—today, embrace the unexpected. What feels different or unusual may be exactly what your spirit has been craving.

Gratitude Mantra

I am grateful for my openness to new ideas and the freedom to embrace life's unexpected adventures.

Sagittarius
28 June 2026

The Aquarius Moon aligns with Jupiter, your ruling planet, boosting optimism, social charm, and expansive ideas. This is one of those days where energy flows smoothly, and opportunities may arise through groups, friendships, or networking. Your words carry influence now, and your positivity inspires others. Sagittarius, you're being reminded that when you share your light, it multiplies. Embrace opportunities to connect, teach, or collaborate—your vision can ripple far wider than you realise.

Gratitude Mantra

I am grateful for the joy and abundance that flow when I share my optimism with others.

Sagittarius
29 June 2026

The Moon moves into Pisces, shifting your energy inward toward emotions, home, and intuition. After days of social activity, you may crave quiet, reflection, or connection with loved ones. Creativity and spirituality are favoured now—writing, art, or meditation may bring peace. Sagittarius, while you thrive on adventure, the universe reminds you that rest and emotional healing are equally important. Give yourself permission to slow down, recharge, and nurture your soul.

Gratitude Mantra

I am grateful for the peace and restoration that come from slowing down and reconnecting with my inner world.

Sagittarius
30 June 2026

The Pisces Moon continues, heightening sensitivity and imagination. You may feel more empathetic, sensing others' needs deeply. While this makes you a compassionate listener, be careful not to absorb their burdens. Spiritual practices, dreams, or creative outlets may provide guidance today. Sagittarius, your adventurous spirit isn't limited to the physical —it also thrives in exploring the mystical. Allow yourself to wander through inner landscapes; insights will come through intuition, not logic.

Gratitude Mantra

I am grateful for my intuition and the guidance it offers through subtle signs and inner wisdom.

July 2026

Sagittarius
1 July 2026

The Pisces Moon harmonises with Pluto, stirring emotional depth and potential for healing. Old feelings may rise, asking for closure or release. This is a chance to let go of burdens you've carried too long. Sagittarius, while you prefer looking forward, freedom sometimes comes from resolving the past. A heartfelt conversation, journaling, or forgiveness ritual may bring transformation. What feels heavy today can become the very thing that sets you free. Honour the process.

Gratitude Mantra

I am grateful for the healing and freedom that come from releasing the past with compassion.

Sagittarius
02 July 2026

The Moon shifts into Aries, reigniting your fire and adventurous spirit. Energy feels bold and dynamic, urging you to take initiative and act on ideas you've been considering. This is a perfect day for creative expression, romance, or starting a new personal project. Your confidence is magnetic, drawing others toward you. Be mindful not to rush or act impulsively, but don't hold back from following your instincts. Sagittarius, this is your cosmic green light—leap toward what excites you most.

Gratitude Mantra

I am grateful for the courage to act boldly and the confidence to follow my instincts.

Sagittarius
03 July 2026

The Aries Moon continues, amplifying your confidence, charisma, and passion. You may feel eager to lead, inspire, or share your vision with others. Your energy is infectious, making it an excellent day for social interactions, creative pursuits, or romance. Be mindful of impatience—others may not move at your pace. Sagittarius, your challenge is to channel this fire productively, turning enthusiasm into purposeful action rather than scattering it in many directions.

Gratitude Mantra

I am grateful for my passion and the ability to channel it into meaningful action.

Sagittarius
04 July 2026

The Moon in Aries forms dynamic aspects, stirring restlessness and a desire for independence. You may crave freedom and resist restrictions, whether in work, relationships, or routines. While this fiery energy empowers you to assert yourself, be mindful of impulsive reactions. Sagittarius, your truth is important, but it shines brightest when expressed with balance and respect. Use today's surge of energy to pursue personal goals, exercise, or creative outlets that channel passion constructively.

Gratitude Mantra

I am grateful for my independence and the freedom to express my authentic self.

Sagittarius
5 July 2026

The Moon moves into Taurus, slowing the pace and grounding your energy. After fiery days, today invites you to focus on stability, comfort, and the simple joys of life. This is a day for enjoying nature, good food, or quality time with loved ones. Practical matters like finances or routines may also require attention. Sagittarius, while you thrive on adventure, this slower pace restores balance and reminds you of the value of consistency.

Gratitude Mantra

I am grateful for the stability and comfort that ground me and support my bigger dreams.

Sagittarius
6 July 2026

The Taurus Moon continues, emphasising patience, persistence, and practicality. You may feel drawn to focus on financial planning, health habits, or long-term projects. While progress feels slower than you'd like, steady effort is building lasting results. Sagittarius, your fire often pushes you toward quick wins, but today the lesson is that consistency is the true key to freedom. Honour small steps—they're carrying you toward the future you desire.

Gratitude Mantra

I am grateful for my patience and the steady progress that creates lasting success.

Sagittarius
7 July 2026

The Taurus Moon harmonises with Saturn, highlighting discipline and responsibility. You may feel motivated to commit to your long-term goals and prove your reliability. Authority figures or mentors may notice your effort, offering recognition or guidance. Sagittarius, this is a reminder that freedom is built on the foundation of responsibility. Don't underestimate the satisfaction that comes from discipline—it empowers you to pursue your dreams without fear. Success today is measured by persistence.

Gratitude Mantra

I am grateful for the discipline and commitment that support my freedom and growth.

Sagittarius
8 July 2026

The Moon enters Gemini, lightening the mood and sparking curiosity. After days of focus and discipline, you're ready to explore, connect, and learn. Social interactions feel lively, and conversations may open new opportunities. Your restless spirit thrives under this influence, but be careful not to scatter your energy across too many directions. Sagittarius, choose the connections and ideas that align with your greater vision. Inspiration arrives when you're open yet discerning.

Gratitude Mantra

I am grateful for the curiosity and connections that broaden my perspective and enrich my path.

Sagittarius
09 July 2026

The Gemini Moon continues, amplifying your need for variety, conversation, and exploration. You may feel pulled in several directions, juggling multiple projects, conversations, or social invitations. While this energy excites your adventurous nature, be mindful of scattering your focus. Not everything requires your immediate attention—choose the paths that genuinely resonate. Sagittarius, your curiosity is a gift, but it flourishes most when guided by intention. Use today to learn, connect, and brainstorm, but keep your eyes on the bigger picture.

Gratitude Mantra

I am grateful for my curiosity and the clarity to focus it on what truly excites me.

Sagittarius
10 July 2026

The Gemini Moon squares Neptune, creating potential confusion in communication or planning. Misunderstandings may arise, or you may feel uncertain about the path forward. Avoid making important decisions without all the details—clarity will come later. Instead, lean into creative and spiritual pursuits where imagination is an asset. Sagittarius, your optimism helps you rise above uncertainty, but patience is key. Trust that today's haze is temporary, and insight will return when the time is right.

Gratitude Mantra

I am grateful for the patience to trust clarity will come when I need it.

Sagittarius
11 July 2026

The Moon moves into Cancer, turning your focus inward toward emotions, home, and family. You may feel more sensitive than usual, craving nurturing and connection. This is a day for slowing down, cooking, or simply creating a cosy atmosphere. Old feelings could surface, giving you the chance to heal or strengthen bonds. Sagittarius, while adventure fuels you, your spirit also needs grounding in love and emotional security. Today, focus on replenishing your heart.

Gratitude Mantra

I am grateful for the comfort of home and the emotional nourishment that sustains me.

Sagittarius
12 July 2026

The Cancer Moon continues, highlighting empathy and emotional awareness. You may find yourself supporting loved ones or reflecting on your own emotional needs. While you often prefer to keep moving, Sagittarius, the cosmos reminds you that stillness can be deeply healing. Take time for journaling, meditation, or conversations that nurture connection. Compassion is your superpower today—use it to bring comfort and understanding to both yourself and others.

Gratitude Mantra

I am grateful for my compassion and the healing it brings to myself and those I love.

Sagittarius
13 July 2026

The Cancer Moon opposes Pluto, bringing intensity in emotional or relationship matters. Old wounds or hidden truths may rise to the surface, demanding your attention. While this energy feels heavy, it's also transformative. Sagittarius, you're being asked to face what's been buried so you can move forward lighter. Don't shy away—transformation requires courage. By leaning into honesty and vulnerability, you gain freedom and clarity. Use this energy for deep healing and renewal.

Gratitude Mantra

I am grateful for my courage to face emotional truths and the growth they bring.

Sagittarius
14 July 2026

The Moon enters Leo, reigniting your adventurous spark and reminding you of your natural confidence. Energy turns playful, creative, and enthusiastic. This is a wonderful day to express yourself boldly, pursue romance, or start a project that excites you. Your charisma draws people in, and opportunities may appear through social interactions. Sagittarius, your fire is magnetic today—use it to shine, inspire, and spread joy wherever you go.

Gratitude Mantra

I am grateful for my confidence and the joy it inspires in both myself and others.

Sagittarius
15 July 2026

The Leo Moon continues, amplifying your leadership qualities and creative fire. You may feel called to take centre stage, whether in work, social settings, or personal projects. Your energy uplifts others, but remember that true leadership also empowers those around you. Sagittarius, your boldness inspires growth, but humility strengthens your impact. Today is a chance to balance confidence with compassion, making your influence even more powerful. Step up, but also lift others with you.

Gratitude Mantra

I am grateful for my ability to lead with both confidence and compassion.

Sagittarius
16 July 2026

The Leo Moon continues, encouraging you to live boldly, take risks, and embrace joy. This is a day to celebrate your creativity, passions, and playful side. Opportunities may arise for romance, artistic pursuits, or social interactions that lift your spirit. Sagittarius, your adventurous fire is at its peak, and people are drawn to your light. Be mindful of overextending your energy—choose what truly excites you. When you follow joy authentically, you attract abundance naturally. Today is about shining unapologetically and letting others bask in your warmth.

Gratitude Mantra

I am grateful for my courage to live joyfully and share my light with others.

Sagittarius
17 July 2026

The Moon shifts into Virgo, slowing the pace and bringing focus to work, health, and practical responsibilities. After fiery Leo days, this grounding influence helps you organise and refine. It's an excellent day to tidy, plan, or make steady progress on projects. Sagittarius, while discipline may feel restrictive, it actually supports your adventurous freedom. When your routines and responsibilities are in order, you have more space to chase what excites you. Balance fire with focus today—it will strengthen your path forward.

Gratitude Mantra

I am grateful for the grounding energy that supports my freedom and future adventures.

Sagittarius
18 July 2026

The Virgo Moon continues, highlighting productivity, organisation, and self-improvement. You may feel called to refine your daily habits or focus on details you've been avoiding. Though not as thrilling as adventure, these tasks create clarity and peace of mind. Sagittarius, your fiery energy often seeks the big picture, but today the magic lies in small, consistent steps. Honour your responsibilities and your health—you'll feel stronger and more energised for the journeys ahead.

Gratitude Mantra

I am grateful for the clarity and strength that come from tending to details with care.

Sagittarius
19 July 2026

The Virgo Moon aligns with Uranus, bringing unexpected changes to routines, work, or health. Plans may shift suddenly, requiring you to adapt quickly. Instead of resisting, embrace the shake-up—Sagittarius, flexibility is one of your greatest strengths. A surprising idea or opportunity may emerge, offering a new way to approach daily life. What first feels disruptive could become liberating. Trust the universe's timing; sometimes detours are hidden shortcuts to where you're meant to go.

Gratitude Mantra

I am grateful for my adaptability and the new opportunities that come from unexpected changes.

Sagittarius
20 July 2026

The Moon enters Libra, turning your focus to partnerships, balance, and harmony. Relationships of all kinds come into the spotlight, and you're encouraged to seek fairness and cooperation. Conversations flow more easily today, making it a good time to resolve conflicts or build bridges. Sagittarius, you thrive on independence, but connection is equally important for your growth. Today's lesson is to honour your truth while respecting others'. Partnership is not restriction—it's expansion when aligned with the right people.

Gratitude Mantra

I am grateful for the balance of independence and connection that strengthens my relationships.

Sagittarius
21 July 2026

The Libra Moon continues, amplifying your role as peacemaker and collaborator. You may find yourself mediating, supporting friends, or working closely with others on shared goals. Your honesty, paired with optimism, makes you a natural leader in group settings. Sagittarius, this is a day to focus on cooperation and diplomacy, but don't sacrifice your authenticity in the process. When you balance honesty with kindness, your words heal and inspire. Relationships today can grow deeper and stronger.

Gratitude Mantra

I am grateful for the harmony and cooperation that enrich my connections.

Sagittarius
22 July 2026

The Sun enters Leo, boosting your fire and confidence, while the Libra Moon highlights relationships. This combination encourages you to express yourself boldly in love, partnerships, and creative ventures. Sagittarius, your adventurous spirit thrives under Leo's influence—you'll feel eager to explore, lead, and shine. Relationships benefit from your honesty and enthusiasm, but be mindful of dominating conversations. Share your fire generously; when you uplift others, your own light burns even brighter. This is a day to celebrate both individuality and connection.

Gratitude Mantra

I am grateful for the confidence to shine and the love that grows when I share my light.

Sagittarius
23 July 2026

The Moon enters Scorpio, intensifying emotions and sharpening your intuition. You may feel drawn to explore subjects beneath the surface—hidden truths, unspoken feelings, or deeper aspects of yourself. This is a day for transformation, reflection, and honesty. While intensity may feel uncomfortable, it offers liberation. Sagittarius, your adventurous spirit prefers lightness, but true freedom sometimes requires facing shadows. Don't resist the depth—it has lessons to teach. Journaling, meditation, or vulnerable conversations may bring breakthroughs and healing.

Gratitude Mantra

I am grateful for the courage to face deep truths and the transformation they bring.

Sagittarius
24 July 2026

The Scorpio Moon continues, highlighting themes of intimacy, trust, and transformation. Relationships may feel more intense, as hidden dynamics or old issues surface. While this can feel heavy, it's an opportunity to deepen bonds through honesty. Financial matters may also come into focus, prompting you to rethink shared resources or long-term strategies. Sagittarius, your gift of truth-telling can heal when used with compassion. Today, your fire combines with depth to create powerful growth.

Gratitude Mantra

I am grateful for the strength to transform challenges into opportunities for deeper connection and growth.

Sagittarius
25 July 2026

The Moon enters Sagittarius, lifting your spirit and reigniting optimism. After days of intensity, you're ready to explore, laugh, and expand. Travel, learning, or simply stepping outside your comfort zone feels energising now. Your charisma shines, and opportunities may appear through chance encounters or bold decisions. Sagittarius, this is your natural rhythm—curiosity and adventure. Follow your instincts, say yes to opportunities, and let your fire inspire those around you. The universe rewards your courage today.

Gratitude Mantra

I am grateful for my adventurous nature and the opportunities it brings to expand my horizons.

Sagittarius
26 July 2026

The Sagittarius Moon continues, amplifying your energy, confidence, and passion. This is a day to pursue personal goals, share your vision, and celebrate your individuality. Your enthusiasm inspires others, but be mindful not to overwhelm them with your pace. Sagittarius, your gift lies in living authentically and encouraging others to do the same. Bold actions and new experiences are favoured now—take steps toward the dreams that light your spirit.

Gratitude Mantra

I am grateful for my confidence and the freedom to live authentically and boldly.

Sagittarius
27 July 2026

The Sagittarius Moon harmonises with Jupiter, your ruling planet, creating a day of luck, growth, and expansion. Opportunities may arrive through learning, travel, or new connections. Your optimism is magnetic, and others are drawn to your adventurous nature. Sagittarius, this is a reminder that when you follow your joy, abundance flows naturally. Be open to invitations, explore possibilities, and trust your instincts—they're leading you to something meaningful. Today is about embracing possibility with excitement.

Gratitude Mantra

I am grateful for the abundance that flows when I follow joy and trust my instincts.

Sagittarius
28 July 2026

The Moon shifts into Capricorn, grounding your fire and focusing you on long-term goals. After adventurous days, it's time to commit to structure and responsibility. Career matters, finances, or health routines may require attention. Sagittarius, while you thrive on freedom, discipline is what ensures lasting success. Think of today as building the scaffolding that supports your future adventures. Hard work today will pay off in lasting rewards. Balance fire with focus for powerful progress.

Gratitude Mantra

I am grateful for the discipline that builds strong foundations for my dreams.

Sagittarius
29 July 2026

The Capricorn Moon continues, reminding you of the value of perseverance. You may feel called to prove your reliability, take on responsibility, or show leadership. Recognition for your efforts may come, but the true reward is knowing you're building something meaningful. Sagittarius, success isn't just about excitement—it's about persistence and dedication. Trust that every step forward, no matter how small, contributes to your larger vision. Today's lesson: consistency fuels freedom.

Gratitude Mantra

I am grateful for my perseverance and the steady progress that creates lasting success.

Sagittarius
30 July 2026

The Capricorn Moon aligns with Uranus, bringing sudden changes to routines, work, or responsibilities. Plans may shift unexpectedly, forcing you to adapt quickly. While disruptions can feel inconvenient, they also spark breakthroughs and innovative solutions. Sagittarius, your adventurous spirit thrives when life surprises you—today's shake-up is an opportunity to see things from a fresh perspective. Be flexible, open-minded, and ready to pivot. What first feels like a detour may turn into a shortcut toward progress. Trust the cosmic redirection.

Gratitude Mantra

I am grateful for my adaptability and the growth that comes from life's surprises.

Sagittarius
31 July 2026

The Moon enters Aquarius, highlighting friendships, community, and shared ideas. You may feel inspired to collaborate with others, brainstorm innovative solutions, or get involved in social causes. Conversations with like-minded people expand your vision and open doors to opportunities. Sagittarius, your fire adds enthusiasm to any group effort, and today you're reminded that your light grows brighter when shared. Surround yourself with people who uplift and inspire you—together, you can create meaningful change.

Gratitude Mantra

I am grateful for the connections and communities that inspire and expand my vision.

August
2026

Sagittarius
01 August 2026

The Aquarius Moon continues, encouraging originality and freedom. You may feel restless under routine, craving new experiences or unconventional approaches. Technology, networking, or progressive ideas may play an important role today. Sagittarius, your role is to embrace curiosity and explore paths that break tradition. Your adventurous nature thrives when you're not confined—lean into the unusual. What feels unconventional today could become tomorrow's opportunity. Trust that your uniqueness is your greatest strength.

Gratitude Mantra

I am grateful for my originality and the courage to explore new ways of living and creating.

Sagittarius
2 August 2026

The Aquarius Moon harmonises with Jupiter, boosting optimism, social charm, and expansive ideas. Opportunities may arise through groups, friendships, or chance conversations. This is a day when your adventurous spirit blends beautifully with collective energy—your positivity inspires others and attracts support. Sagittarius, when you share your enthusiasm, it ripples outward, creating connections that benefit everyone. Trust in collaboration; the universe is reminding you that success is rarely a solo journey. Today, your light uplifts many.

Gratitude Mantra

I am grateful for the joy and abundance that flow when I share my light with others.

Sagittarius
3 August 2026

The Moon enters Pisces, turning your focus inward toward emotions, intuition, and home. After social energy, you may crave rest, reflection, and deeper connection with loved ones. Creative outlets, meditation, or time spent in nature will soothe your spirit. Sagittarius, while you thrive on adventure, you also need moments of stillness to refuel. Today is about honouring your emotional world and finding wisdom in quiet spaces. Trust your intuition—it's guiding you gently now.

Gratitude Mantra

I am grateful for the peace and wisdom that come from quiet reflection.

Sagittarius
4 August 2026

The Pisces Moon continues, heightening empathy and imagination. You may feel more sensitive to others' needs, making compassion essential. Be careful not to take on burdens that aren't yours—boundaries keep your energy strong. Spiritual practices, dreams, or creative activities may bring insight today. Sagittarius, your adventurous fire can also explore inner landscapes—journeys of the soul bring as much discovery as those in the outer world. Listen closely; answers come in whispers now.

Gratitude Mantra

I am grateful for my compassion and the guidance my intuition brings.

Sagittarius
5 August 2026

The Pisces Moon aligns with Pluto, encouraging emotional healing and release. Old wounds or hidden feelings may surface, but this is an opportunity to let go and transform. Sagittarius, you often prefer to look forward, but the cosmos reminds you that freedom comes from clearing the past. Vulnerability brings strength today—don't fear it. By embracing honesty with yourself and others, you create space for renewal. Healing now sets you free for future adventures.

Gratitude Mantra

I am grateful for the healing that comes from releasing the past with honesty and compassion.

Sagittarius
06 August 2026

The Moon moves into Aries, reigniting your fiery energy and zest for adventure. Confidence surges, and you may feel the urge to take bold action, whether in creative pursuits, personal projects, or romance. Your enthusiasm is magnetic, inspiring those around you. Be mindful, however, of impatience—rushing may cause unnecessary mistakes. Sagittarius, this is your cosmic invitation to act on what excites you, but do so with intention. When you channel passion constructively, incredible progress is possible today.

Gratitude Mantra

I am grateful for the fire within me and the courage to channel it into bold, purposeful action.

Sagittarius
07 August 2026

The Aries Moon continues, boosting passion, leadership, and determination. You're eager to step forward and claim your space, whether in relationships, work, or creative projects. Your natural charisma draws people in, but ensure you don't overshadow others—true leadership uplifts as well as inspires. Sagittarius, you thrive when you're moving quickly, but today's lesson is to balance speed with awareness. When you temper action with wisdom, your fire becomes unstoppable.

Gratitude Mantra

I am grateful for my courage to lead with passion and inspire others along the way.

Sagittarius
08 August 2026

With the Aries Moon forming tense aspects, you may feel impatient or restless if progress is slower than expected. Frustrations could arise, especially if others don't match your pace. Instead of reacting impulsively, channel excess energy into physical activity, problem-solving, or creativity. Sagittarius, your adventurous spirit loves movement, but patience is part of the journey too. By embracing both energy and restraint, you'll find strength and clarity. This is a day to practice balance.

Gratitude Mantra

I am grateful for my resilience and the balance of energy and patience that guide me.

Sagittarius
09 August 2026

The Moon shifts into Taurus, slowing the tempo and grounding your fire. This is a day to focus on stability, comfort, and practical matters like finances, health, or routines. After fiery Aries energy, the cosmos asks you to pace yourself and enjoy simple pleasures. Sagittarius, your adventurous soul often looks outward, but today you'll find joy in slowing down and appreciating what's steady. Grounding doesn't limit you—it supports your ability to soar higher.

Gratitude Mantra

I am grateful for the grounding energy that steadies me and the simple joys that enrich my life.

Sagittarius
10 August 2026

The Taurus Moon continues, emphasising persistence and consistency. You may feel called to commit to long-term goals, financial planning, or health habits. Progress may feel slow, but don't mistake it for stagnation—steady steps today create real, lasting results. Sagittarius, your nature craves speed and variety, but the universe reminds you that sustainability is key. Honour routines and commit to discipline; they'll fuel your freedom tomorrow. Stability today is a gift to your future self.

Gratitude Mantra

I am grateful for the persistence and steady effort that build a secure and abundant future.

Sagittarius
11 August 2026

The Taurus Moon aligns with Saturn, strengthening focus and responsibility. You may feel motivated to take commitments seriously and put in the effort needed for success. This is a day for discipline—work, finances, or projects benefit from your attention. Recognition may come from authority figures or mentors, affirming your reliability. Sagittarius, you thrive on freedom, but responsibility is what makes freedom sustainable. Embrace today's energy—it helps you build the foundation for your biggest adventures.

Gratitude Mantra

I am grateful for the discipline and responsibility that support my long-term dreams.

Sagittarius
12 August 2026

The Moon enters Gemini, bringing curiosity, lively energy, and a flurry of ideas. Conversations, socialising, and learning are highlighted now. You may feel pulled in multiple directions, eager to explore everything at once. While variety excites you, Sagittarius, the lesson today is focus—don't scatter your fire too thin. Choose the ideas and connections that resonate most with your bigger vision. Inspiration is abundant; clarity comes when you channel it wisely.

Gratitude Mantra

I am grateful for my curiosity and the clarity to focus it on what aligns with my vision.

Sagittarius
13 August 2026

The Gemini Moon continues, filling your day with curiosity, conversation, and exploration. Your mind is buzzing, and opportunities for learning or networking are strong. You may feel pulled in multiple directions—emails, social invites, or fresh ideas popping up at once. While exciting, this can scatter your energy if you're not careful. Sagittarius, your challenge is to prioritise: focus on what feels aligned with your bigger picture. Use this mental energy for brainstorming, journaling, or exploring new topics that fuel your growth.

Gratitude Mantra

I am grateful for my curious mind and the inspiration it brings when I explore with purpose.

Sagittarius
14 August 2026

The Gemini Moon squares Neptune, creating a fog around conversations, planning, or decision-making. Miscommunication or unclear information may arise, so avoid finalising agreements or making big choices today. Instead, lean into creativity, imagination, and intuition. Sagittarius, your adventurous spirit thrives on clarity, but sometimes uncertainty teaches you patience and trust. Focus on spiritual practices, art, or journaling rather than chasing immediate answers. Clarity will return soon—don't rush it.

Gratitude Mantra

I am grateful for my patience and the trust that clarity arrives in its own perfect timing.

Sagittarius
15 August 2026

The Moon shifts into Cancer, turning your energy inward toward home, family, and emotional needs. You may crave comfort, nurturing, or time spent with loved ones. Old feelings may surface, offering an opportunity for healing or deeper connection. Sagittarius, while you thrive on travel and expansion, you also need grounding in emotional safety. Today is about creating a sanctuary, whether through a warm conversation, self-care, or tending to your space. Honour your heart as much as your mind.

Gratitude Mantra

I am grateful for the love and comfort that nourish my heart and soul.

Sagittarius
16 August 2026

The Cancer Moon continues, amplifying empathy and intuition. You may feel sensitive to the moods of others, which makes compassion important. Be mindful, though, not to absorb their burdens—boundaries matter too. This is a good day for reflection, family connections, or practices that soothe your emotional world. Sagittarius, sometimes the greatest adventure is within—today, honour your inner landscapes. Emotional awareness strengthens your fire and makes your journey more balanced and wise.

Gratitude Mantra

I am grateful for my compassion and the strength that comes from honouring my emotional needs.

Sagittarius
17 August 2026

The Cancer Moon opposes Pluto, stirring intensity in relationships or family dynamics. Power struggles or buried emotions may surface, demanding honesty. While uncomfortable, this energy helps release what no longer serves you. Sagittarius, you prefer to look forward, but sometimes the past must be acknowledged to move freely into the future. Use this as a chance to transform, heal, and let go. Freedom often begins with emotional release. Be courageous—it will set you lighter.

Gratitude Mantra

I am grateful for my courage to face intensity and the freedom that comes from emotional release.

Sagittarius
18 August 2026

The Moon enters Leo, reigniting your confidence, joy, and adventurous fire. Creativity, romance, and self-expression are highlighted today. You may feel called to step into the spotlight, pursue passions, or simply enjoy life's pleasures. Your enthusiasm is magnetic, inspiring others around you. Sagittarius, this is your reminder that joy is a form of wisdom—when you live boldly, you guide others to do the same. Celebrate your uniqueness and let your fire shine brightly today.

Gratitude Mantra

I am grateful for my confidence and the joy that inspires me to live boldly.

Sagittarius
19 August 2026

The Leo Moon continues, fuelling your leadership and creative expression. You may feel eager to take centre stage, whether in personal projects, work, or social settings. Your boldness attracts admiration, but remember to balance it with humility. Sagittarius, true leadership empowers others as much as it inspires. Today is a chance to shine while lifting others alongside you. Be authentic, generous, and joyful—your energy will ripple widely.

Gratitude Mantra

I am grateful for my ability to shine with authenticity and inspire others through my light.

Sagittarius
20 August 2026

The Leo Moon aligns with Jupiter, your ruling planet, filling the day with optimism, joy, and confidence. Opportunities may arise in love, creativity, or social life, and your charisma is at its peak. This is a wonderful time for celebrations, bold actions, or simply indulging in fun. Sagittarius, your adventurous fire shines brightly now, reminding you that life is meant to be enjoyed. Be generous with your laughter and spirit—it will ripple far beyond you, inspiring others.

Gratitude Mantra

I am grateful for the joy and abundance that flow when I live boldly and share my light.

Sagittarius
21 August 2026

The Moon shifts into Virgo, grounding yesterday's fire and directing your attention toward details, routines, and responsibilities. You may feel called to get organised, refine projects, or tend to health and practical matters. While this energy may feel slower than you prefer, Sagittarius, it's necessary to balance fire with focus. Think of today as maintenance—strengthening the structures that support your adventurous lifestyle. Progress may not feel dramatic, but it's meaningful and long-lasting.

Gratitude Mantra

I am grateful for the grounding energy that helps me refine my path and strengthen my foundation.

Sagittarius
22 August 2026

The Virgo Moon continues, emphasising productivity and problem-solving. You may notice small details that you've overlooked recently, and this awareness can help you improve systems or routines. While your adventurous heart longs for excitement, Sagittarius, today's gift is efficiency. By tending to the little things, you create clarity and space for future adventures. Don't dismiss the power of order—it frees you to move boldly when opportunities arise. Practical progress today supports bigger dreams tomorrow.

Gratitude Mantra

I am grateful for the clarity and efficiency that come from tending to life's details.

Sagittarius
23 August 2026

The Sun enters Virgo, shining a light on organisation, discipline, and service. Over the next month, you're encouraged to refine routines, care for your health, and focus on meaningful daily habits. Today, the energy is perfect for planning and creating structure that supports long-term goals. Sagittarius, while structure may not feel thrilling, it's the foundation that sustains your fire. Consider how your daily choices shape your future. Aligning action with intention will bring strength and freedom.

Gratitude Mantra

I am grateful for the discipline and structure that support my growth and dreams.

Sagittarius
24 August 2026

The Virgo Moon aligns with Uranus, sparking sudden changes in routines or unexpected insights about health, work, or daily life. While disruptions may feel inconvenient at first, they hold the potential for liberation. Sagittarius, you thrive when life surprises you—today, embrace the unexpected. A new approach or fresh idea could transform the way you handle responsibilities. Stay open and flexible; what shifts now may prove to be the breakthrough you didn't know you needed.

Gratitude Mantra

I am grateful for the surprises that bring fresh perspectives and opportunities for growth.

Sagittarius
25 August 2026

The Moon moves into Libra, turning your focus toward relationships, harmony, and balance. Connections of all kinds feel highlighted now, and you may feel called to compromise, collaborate, or restore peace in a partnership. Sagittarius, you thrive on independence, but today reminds you that cooperation strengthens your path. Seek fairness without losing authenticity. Partnership is not a limitation—it's expansion when aligned with the right people. This is a day for kindness and diplomacy.

Gratitude Mantra

I am grateful for the harmony and balance that enrich my relationships.

Sagittarius
26 August 2026

The Libra Moon continues, encouraging compromise, fairness, and connection. You may find yourself in the role of peacemaker, offering wisdom and optimism to resolve conflicts or support others. This is a good day for creative collaborations or building bridges where tension has lingered. Sagittarius, your gift lies in blending truth with tact. Speak with honesty but temper it with compassion—your words today can heal, uplift, and inspire. Use them with intention.

Gratitude Mantra

I am grateful for the wisdom to speak truth with compassion and create harmony.

Sagittarius
27 August 2026

The Libra Moon aligns with Pluto, bringing depth and transformation to your relationships. Conversations may feel more intense, and you could uncover hidden dynamics or unspoken truths. While this may feel uncomfortable, it's a chance to heal and strengthen bonds through honesty. Sagittarius, you often prefer to keep things light, but today's energy asks for depth and vulnerability. By leaning into truth, you open the door to more authentic and rewarding connections. Transformation in love, friendships, or partnerships is possible if you embrace honesty with compassion.

Gratitude Mantra

I am grateful for the courage to embrace truth and the transformation it brings to my relationships.

Sagittarius
28 August 2026

The Moon shifts into Scorpio, amplifying emotions and sharpening your intuition. You may feel drawn to introspection, spiritual practices, or exploring hidden aspects of yourself. Scorpio energy pushes you to go deeper, revealing truths that can no longer be ignored. Sagittarius, while you love adventure in the outer world, today's journey is inward. Don't shy away from intensity—it offers healing and wisdom. Journaling, meditation, or meaningful conversations may bring profound clarity and renewal.

Gratitude Mantra

I am grateful for my willingness to dive deep and the healing that follows.

Sagittarius
29 August 2026

The Scorpio Moon continues, intensifying emotions and highlighting themes of trust, intimacy, and transformation. Relationships may feel magnetic yet demanding, as deeper issues surface. Financial matters linked to shared resources could also come into focus. Sagittarius, today calls for honesty and courage—avoid escapism and face what arises. Transformation often feels uncomfortable but always leads to liberation. This is your opportunity to release old patterns and create space for authentic growth in love, money, and self-awareness.

Gratitude Mantra

I am grateful for my courage to release old patterns and embrace transformation.

Sagittarius
30 August 2026

The Moon enters Sagittarius, lifting your spirit and reigniting your optimism. After days of emotional depth, you're ready to expand again—exploring, learning, and seeking adventure. Confidence flows naturally, and opportunities may arise through travel, studies, or spontaneous connections. Sagittarius, this is your element: freedom, joy, and curiosity. Follow your instincts and say yes to experiences that excite you. Your enthusiasm inspires others, and your fire lights up every space you enter today.

Gratitude Mantra

I am grateful for my adventurous spirit and the opportunities it attracts.

Sagittarius
31 August 2026

The Sagittarius Moon continues, amplifying your charisma and adventurous drive. This is an excellent day for pursuing personal goals, making bold decisions, or simply enjoying life's journey. Your optimism is magnetic, drawing people and opportunities toward you. Be mindful of scattering your fire—channel it into what matters most. Sagittarius, when you align your adventurous spirit with purpose, your energy becomes unstoppable. Celebrate your uniqueness and step boldly into opportunities that align with your heart.

Gratitude Mantra

I am grateful for my confidence and the freedom to pursue opportunities that align with my truth.

September 2026

Sagittarius
01 September 2026

The Sagittarius Moon aligns with Jupiter, your ruling planet, blessing you with luck, growth, and expansion. This is a day of abundance, optimism, and possibility. New doors may open through travel, education, or chance encounters. Your words carry influence, and your positivity inspires others. Sagittarius, the universe is reminding you that when you live authentically, opportunities flow easily. Share your vision boldly today—the ripple effect could extend further than you imagine.

Gratitude Mantra

I am grateful for the abundance and opportunities that flow when I live authentically and share my vision.

Sagittarius
02 September 2026

The Moon moves into Capricorn, grounding your energy and shifting focus toward responsibility, career, and long-term planning. After fiery Sagittarian days, this is a reminder that discipline sustains freedom. Use today to commit to practical steps, review finances, or focus on your goals with determination. Sagittarius, while structure can feel restrictive, it actually empowers you to live adventurously without fear. Think of today as the framework that will hold your future expansion.

Gratitude Mantra

I am grateful for the discipline and focus that support my long-term freedom and success.

Sagittarius
03 September 2026

The Capricorn Moon continues, bringing focus to responsibility, discipline, and long-term stability. You may feel called to commit to your career, finances, or health routines with renewed determination. While this energy can feel heavy compared to your free-spirited nature, it supports your independence in the long run. Sagittarius, freedom is most enjoyable when it's built on a secure foundation. Today's discipline doesn't limit you—it empowers you to chase dreams without worry. See effort now as an investment in your future adventures.

Gratitude Mantra

I am grateful for the discipline that strengthens my foundation and supports my freedom.

Sagittarius
04 September 2026

The Capricorn Moon aligns with Uranus, shaking up routines with unexpected changes or surprising opportunities. What initially feels disruptive may actually redirect you to a better path. Stay flexible and open to innovation, especially in work or financial matters. Sagittarius, you thrive when life surprises you —today's shifts can lead to breakthroughs if you embrace them. Don't resist change; see it as the universe nudging you toward growth and fresh perspectives. Adaptability is your greatest gift now.

Gratitude Mantra

I am grateful for my flexibility and the breakthroughs that come through change.

Sagittarius
05 September 2026

The Moon enters Aquarius, highlighting friendships, collaboration, and social connections. This is a day for teamwork, networking, or exploring innovative ideas with like-minded people. Conversations may spark inspiration and lead to opportunities that expand your vision. Sagittarius, your optimism uplifts groups and inspires collective progress. Don't isolate yourself—your fire is needed in community spaces. Today reminds you that adventure isn't just personal—it grows when shared with others who support and inspire your journey.

Gratitude Mantra

I am grateful for the connections and collaborations that expand my path.

Sagittarius
06 September 2026

The Aquarius Moon continues, encouraging originality, innovation, and freedom. You may crave a break from routine, seeking excitement in new experiences or unconventional approaches. Technology or progressive ideas may play an important role in today's insights. Sagittarius, you're reminded that exploration isn't limited to travel—it can be mental, social, or spiritual. Follow your curiosity, even if it takes you in unexpected directions. Original thinking opens doors to breakthroughs that align with your adventurous spirit.

Gratitude Mantra

I am grateful for my curiosity and the freedom to explore new possibilities.

Sagittarius
07 September 2026

The Aquarius Moon aligns with Jupiter, boosting optimism, charm, and social energy. Opportunities may arise through groups, friendships, or chance encounters that spark inspiration. Sagittarius, your positivity is magnetic today—share your vision and watch how it attracts support and collaboration. You're reminded that abundance often flows through community. Your adventurous spirit combined with collective energy can create momentum for meaningful growth. Be open to invitations and conversations; they may lead to something expansive.

Gratitude Mantra

I am grateful for the abundance and joy that come through community and shared vision.

Sagittarius
08 September 2026

The Moon enters Pisces, shifting your energy toward emotions, intuition, and healing. After social days, you may crave rest, creativity, or connection with loved ones. Sensitivity runs high, so avoid overexposure to negativity. Instead, nurture yourself with music, art, or spiritual practices. Sagittarius, you love adventure, but today the inner journey matters most. Intuition and dreams hold guidance now—listen closely. Stillness may reveal more than constant motion. Honour your need for quiet restoration.

Gratitude Mantra

I am grateful for the peace and wisdom that come from inner reflection and stillness.

Sagittarius
09 September 2026

The Pisces Moon continues, heightening compassion, creativity, and imagination. You may feel drawn to help others, create art, or explore spiritual practices. Be mindful of boundaries—while empathy is a gift, absorbing others' emotions may drain you. Sagittarius, your adventurous fire can also explore the unseen realms of intuition and spirit. Pay attention to dreams or synchronicities today—they may carry guidance for your next steps. Trust the universe is whispering answers.

Gratitude Mantra

I am grateful for my compassion and the intuitive signs that guide my path.

Sagittarius
10 September 2026

The Pisces Moon aligns with Neptune, enhancing intuition, creativity, and sensitivity. This is a day for imagination and spiritual exploration rather than logic-heavy tasks. Pay attention to dreams, synchronicities, or subtle signs—they may hold guidance. While emotions run deep, avoid escapism or overindulgence. Sagittarius, you thrive on adventure, and today the journey is inward. Embrace meditation, journaling, or creative work to channel this dreamy energy productively. Trust your inner compass—it's more accurate than you think.

Gratitude Mantra

I am grateful for the intuitive guidance and creativity that flow when I listen to my inner world.

Sagittarius
11 September 2026

The Moon enters Aries, igniting boldness, action, and renewed motivation. After days of reflection, you're ready to step forward confidently. Energy surges, encouraging you to take risks, launch new projects, or pursue passions. Your enthusiasm inspires others, but be mindful of impatience—slowing down ensures progress is sustainable. Sagittarius, this fiery influence resonates with your adventurous nature. Today is about courage and momentum—lean into opportunities that excite your spirit and trust your instincts fully.

Gratitude Mantra

I am grateful for my courage to take bold steps and the momentum that carries me forward.

Sagittarius
12 September 2026

The Aries Moon continues, amplifying confidence, passion, and charisma. You may feel drawn to leadership roles, romantic pursuits, or creative expression. Your natural spark is magnetic, attracting people and opportunities. But remember, Sagittarius, fire without direction can burn out quickly. Today's lesson is to channel your energy with focus and purpose. Bold action paired with clear intention creates meaningful progress. Don't be afraid to shine—just ensure your brilliance uplifts others as well as yourself.

Gratitude Mantra

I am grateful for my passion and the wisdom to channel it with purpose.

Sagittarius
13 September 2026

The Aries Moon forms tense aspects, stirring restlessness and frustration. You may feel impatient if results don't come quickly or if others can't keep pace. Avoid impulsive decisions or heated words—pause before reacting. Sagittarius, your fire is powerful, but today you're asked to balance it with patience. Physical activity, creativity, or problem-solving can help release excess energy. By practising restraint, you'll discover clarity and strength you didn't know you had.

Gratitude Mantra

I am grateful for my ability to balance fiery energy with patience and wisdom.

Sagittarius
14 September 2026

The Moon enters Taurus, grounding your fiery spirit and encouraging patience. Focus on stability, comfort, and practical matters such as finances or routines. After the intensity of Aries, this slower rhythm helps restore balance. Sagittarius, while you crave adventure, the cosmos reminds you that consistency and grounding create freedom. Take time to enjoy life's simple pleasures—nature, food, or rest. This calm energy supports long-term progress and replenishes your fire.

Gratitude Mantra

I am grateful for the grounding energy that supports my freedom and long-term growth.

Sagittarius
15 September 2026

The Taurus Moon continues, highlighting persistence, responsibility, and building strong foundations. You may feel motivated to commit to long-term projects or review your financial stability. Progress may feel gradual, but it's meaningful. Sagittarius, this is your reminder that adventure and freedom are sustained by security and discipline. Each small step you take today builds the scaffolding for tomorrow's dreams. Celebrate the slow pace—it's carrying you steadily toward expansion.

Gratitude Mantra

I am grateful for the persistence and stability that strengthen my foundation for the future.

Sagittarius
16 September 2026

The Taurus Moon aligns with Pluto, intensifying focus and transformation in practical matters. You may discover a powerful new approach to finances, work, or health habits. This is a day for breakthroughs if you're willing to confront outdated patterns and replace them with strategies that empower you. Sagittarius, though you prefer to keep moving forward, pausing to refine your foundation gives you greater freedom later. Transformation today creates strength for tomorrow's adventures.

Gratitude Mantra

I am grateful for the breakthroughs that come from transforming old patterns into empowering foundations.

Sagittarius
17 September 2026

The Moon enters Gemini, sparking curiosity, conversation, and exploration. Your mind feels lively, and you may be pulled in many directions—emails, social interactions, or fresh ideas all vying for attention. While this excites your adventurous spirit, it risks scattering your focus. Sagittarius, today's challenge is to choose wisely which opportunities to pursue. Communication is highlighted, and your words carry influence, so use them with care. This is a wonderful day for brainstorming, writing, or networking, but don't overcommit. Keep your fire concentrated on what aligns with your bigger vision.

Gratitude Mantra

I am grateful for my curiosity and the wisdom to focus it on what matters most.

Sagittarius
18 September 2026

The Gemini Moon continues, filling your day with mental stimulation and lively interactions. Conversations flow easily, and opportunities may arise through chance encounters or networking. While this is an inspiring time, you may feel restless or overwhelmed by too many options. Sagittarius, your gift lies in seeing the big picture—use it to filter out distractions. Say yes only to what feels meaningful. The universe is reminding you that while variety excites you, clarity and focus create true progress.

Gratitude Mantra

I am grateful for the clarity that helps me prioritise what aligns with my greater purpose.

Sagittarius
19 September 2026

The Gemini Moon squares Saturn, creating tension between curiosity and responsibility. You may feel limited by obligations or frustrated that things aren't moving quickly. Miscommunication or delays could test your patience. Sagittarius, this is a day for persistence—lean into resilience rather than letting obstacles dim your fire. See delays as opportunities to refine your vision and strengthen your resolve. Today's lessons are about patience, discipline, and staying true to your path even when tested.

Gratitude Mantra

I am grateful for my resilience and the patience to stay steady when challenges arise.

Sagittarius
20 September 2026

The Moon enters Cancer, shifting energy toward home, family, and emotional nourishment. You may crave comfort, connection, or a safe space to recharge. Old feelings may resurface, offering healing if acknowledged with honesty. Sagittarius, though you thrive on movement, the universe reminds you of the importance of emotional grounding. Nurture your heart, spend time with loved ones, and honour your inner world. Adventures are brighter when your emotional foundation is strong.

Gratitude Mantra

I am grateful for the love and comfort that ground me and support my spirit.

Sagittarius
21 September 2026

The Cancer Moon continues, amplifying your intuition and sensitivity. You may feel deeply connected to others' emotions, which can strengthen relationships if balanced with boundaries. Creative or spiritual practices are favoured today—music, art, or meditation may bring peace. Sagittarius, your adventurous spirit isn't just about exploring the world—it's about exploring the depths within. Today, emotional honesty and self-compassion will help you grow stronger and more centred for the road ahead.

Gratitude Mantra

I am grateful for my intuition and the compassion that guide me toward deeper understanding.

Sagittarius
22 September 2026

The Cancer Moon opposes Pluto, stirring emotional intensity in relationships or family dynamics. Hidden truths may surface, or old wounds may reopen. While this can feel challenging, it's an opportunity for profound healing and release. Sagittarius, your natural optimism helps you face difficulties with courage. Don't shy away from what arises—embrace it as part of your journey. Transformation often comes through emotional honesty, and today offers you the chance to lighten your load for future adventures.

Gratitude Mantra

I am grateful for the courage to face emotional truths and the freedom that comes from healing.

Sagittarius
23 September 2026

The Moon moves into Leo, lifting your energy with passion, playfulness, and confidence. After emotional Cancer days, you're ready to shine again. This is a wonderful day for creativity, romance, or leadership roles. Your enthusiasm is contagious, and opportunities may arise through bold self-expression. Sagittarius, your adventurous nature thrives under Leo's fire—this is your chance to live boldly and unapologetically. Trust that when you follow joy, abundance follows naturally. Celebrate your uniqueness and inspire others with your light.

Gratitude Mantra

I am grateful for my confidence and the joy that flows when I live authentically.

Sagittarius
24 September 2026

The Leo Moon continues, filling the day with confidence, creativity, and a playful spark. You may feel inspired to take centre stage, whether through work, romance, or personal projects. Your fire is magnetic, drawing people toward you. Sagittarius, this is a chance to shine, but remember that true leadership also uplifts others. Be bold, but also generous with your energy. Celebrate your uniqueness, but leave space for others to express theirs too. Today is about radiating joy while building authentic connections through your light.

Gratitude Mantra

I am grateful for my confidence and my ability to uplift others by sharing my joy.

Sagittarius
25 September 2026

The Leo Moon aligns with Jupiter, your ruling planet, bringing optimism, luck, and expansive energy. This is one of those rare days where opportunities seem to flow effortlessly—romance, creativity, or social connections may sparkle. Sagittarius, your adventurous spirit thrives under this influence, and the cosmos encourages you to dream bigger than usual. Say yes to experiences that light up your heart and soul. Today is about abundance, laughter, and joy—the kind that multiplies when shared with others.

Gratitude Mantra

I am grateful for the abundance and joy that flow when I follow my passions wholeheartedly.

Sagittarius
26 September 2026

The Moon shifts into Virgo, grounding yesterday's fiery energy. Your focus turns to details, routines, and practical tasks. While it may feel less exciting, this energy helps you refine your plans and create order. Sagittarius, your adventurous spirit loves freedom, but freedom is sustainable only when supported by structure. Use today to get organised, tend to responsibilities, or improve daily habits. Think of this as sharpening your tools before the next big adventure.

Gratitude Mantra

I am grateful for the clarity and order that support my freedom and long-term goals.

Sagittarius
27 September 2026

The Virgo Moon continues, encouraging productivity and problem-solving. You may feel motivated to fix, refine, or perfect aspects of your work or personal routines. While perfectionism could creep in, remember that progress matters more than flawless results. Sagittarius, your energy often leaps ahead, but today's lesson is the power of patience and precision. Each small adjustment you make today clears the path for bigger successes tomorrow. Don't underestimate the importance of the little things.

Gratitude Mantra

I am grateful for the progress that comes from patience and small, steady improvements.

Sagittarius
28 September 2026

The Virgo Moon aligns with Uranus, bringing surprises or disruptions to routines. Plans may change suddenly, but flexibility will turn obstacles into opportunities. Innovative solutions may present themselves, especially in work or health matters. Sagittarius, you thrive on variety, and today's shake-up could spark fresh ideas or open unexpected doors. Don't resist change—it's the universe redirecting you to something better. Stay curious and flexible; breakthroughs often hide within disruption.

Gratitude Mantra

I am grateful for my adaptability and the fresh perspectives that change brings.

Sagittarius
29 September 2026

The Moon moves into Libra, turning focus to partnerships, balance, and harmony. Relationships of all kinds—romantic, friendships, or professional—become highlighted. Today is about compromise and cooperation, but without losing authenticity. Sagittarius, you value freedom, yet true growth often comes through meaningful connections. Seek balance, not sacrifice. Conversations flow smoothly, making this a good day for resolving conflicts or strengthening bonds. Authentic collaboration brings harmony and expansion.

Gratitude Mantra

I am grateful for the balance and harmony that strengthen my connections.

Sagittarius
30 September 2026

The Libra Moon continues, encouraging diplomacy, fairness, and connection. You may find yourself playing the role of mediator, using your honesty and optimism to guide conversations toward peace. Collaborative projects thrive under this influence, and relationships can deepen when approached with patience and compassion. Sagittarius, your truth is a gift, but today it shines best when softened with tact. Let your words inspire, not overwhelm. Authenticity and kindness together create harmony and progress.

Gratitude Mantra

I am grateful for my ability to speak truth with compassion and create harmony in my relationships.

October 2026

Sagittarius
01 October 2026

The Libra Moon aligns with Pluto, deepening emotions and relationships. Conversations may carry more weight, and you could feel compelled to confront truths you've been avoiding. While intensity may feel unsettling, it offers transformation. Sagittarius, you often prefer to keep life light, but today's cosmic energy asks you to embrace depth. Honest, vulnerable exchanges can heal and strengthen bonds. Trust that leaning into honesty will ultimately bring freedom. Use this energy to clear old emotional baggage and step into authentic connection.

Gratitude Mantra

I am grateful for the courage to face deep truths and the freedom that honesty brings.

Sagittarius
02 October 2026

The Moon enters Scorpio, turning your attention inward and intensifying emotions. You may feel more reflective, craving solitude or meaningful conversations. Themes of transformation, intimacy, and self-awareness are highlighted. Sagittarius, your adventurous spirit thrives on discovery, and today the cosmos directs you toward inner exploration. Don't shy away from what feels heavy—it carries the keys to growth. Journaling, meditation, or time in quiet reflection will reveal insights that help you step into your power.

Gratitude Mantra

I am grateful for my willingness to explore within and the wisdom that self-discovery brings.

Sagittarius
03 October 2026

The Scorpio Moon continues, stirring intensity in relationships and uncovering hidden truths. You may feel more sensitive to undercurrents, noticing dynamics others overlook. While this can feel overwhelming, it's an opportunity for clarity. Sagittarius, your honesty is a gift—use it to address issues directly but with compassion. Transformation in love, finances, or personal growth is possible if you release resistance. Today invites you to embrace depth and trust that change brings empowerment.

Gratitude Mantra

I am grateful for the transformation that comes when I embrace depth with honesty and courage.

Sagittarius
04 October 2026

The Moon enters Sagittarius, lifting your energy and reigniting optimism. After days of intensity, you're ready to expand outward again—exploring, learning, and embracing new adventures. Your confidence and enthusiasm attract opportunities, whether through travel, study, or spontaneous connections. This is your natural rhythm, Sagittarius: seeking freedom, joy, and truth. Say yes to experiences that excite you, and let your fire inspire others. The cosmos is reminding you that your adventurous spirit is your greatest gift.

Gratitude Mantra

I am grateful for my adventurous spirit and the joy it brings into my life.

Sagittarius
05 October 2026

The Sagittarius Moon continues, amplifying your fire, charisma, and drive. This is a day to pursue personal goals, speak your truth, and share your vision with confidence. Your optimism inspires others, but take care not to scatter your energy across too many directions. Sagittarius, when you align passion with purpose, your fire becomes unstoppable. Use today's expansive energy to take bold steps toward dreams that matter most to your heart.

Gratitude Mantra

I am grateful for my confidence and the focus that channels my passion into meaningful progress.

Sagittarius
06 October 2026

The Sagittarius Moon aligns with Jupiter, your ruling planet, creating a powerful day for expansion, luck, and growth. Opportunities may appear through learning, travel, or chance encounters, and your adventurous spirit is ready to leap. This is one of those days when the universe seems to align in your favour. Sagittarius, be bold and trust your instincts—doors are opening for you now. Celebrate this wave of abundance by saying yes to experiences that light up your soul.

Gratitude Mantra

I am grateful for the abundance and opportunities that flow when I trust my adventurous spirit.

Sagittarius
07 October 2026

The Moon shifts into Capricorn, grounding your fiery energy and focusing attention on responsibility and long-term goals. After expansive days, it's time to commit to structure and discipline. Career matters, financial planning, or health routines benefit from your focus. Sagittarius, you sometimes resist structure, but today you'll see how it empowers you to live more freely in the long run. This is about building the foundation that sustains your adventurous lifestyle. Steady steps taken now will secure tomorrow's freedom.

Gratitude Mantra

I am grateful for the structure and discipline that strengthen my future adventures.

Sagittarius
08 October 2026

The Capricorn Moon continues, highlighting persistence, focus, and responsibility. You may feel the weight of duties, especially in work or financial matters, but this is an opportunity to demonstrate reliability. Sagittarius, while your spirit craves freedom, the cosmos reminds you that structure sustains adventure. Use today to commit to long-term goals or take steady steps on projects that require endurance. Small achievements will bring satisfaction now. Think of this as building scaffolding for your future dreams—the adventure will be richer because of today's discipline.

Gratitude Mantra

I am grateful for my persistence and the steady progress that secures my freedom.

Sagittarius
09 October 2026

The Capricorn Moon harmonises with Uranus, sparking sudden changes or innovative solutions in work, finances, or health routines. Disruptions may initially feel inconvenient, but they open doors to new approaches. Sagittarius, your adaptable spirit thrives when life surprises you—today, flexibility is your greatest strength. Welcome shifts as opportunities to refresh stagnant areas of your life. The cosmos is encouraging you to think outside the box and find freedom in unexpected pathways. What feels like a detour may be destiny's shortcut.

Gratitude Mantra

I am grateful for my adaptability and the freedom found in unexpected change.

Sagittarius
10 October 2026

The Moon enters Aquarius, bringing focus to friendships, community, and collaboration. Social energy flows easily, and you may feel inspired by conversations with like-minded people. Opportunities may arise through teamwork or networking, and your enthusiasm uplifts those around you. Sagittarius, while you often chase solo adventures, today reminds you that growth multiplies when shared. Your fire adds energy to any group you join—contribute openly but also listen. Inspiration is found in collective wisdom and shared goals.

Gratitude Mantra

I am grateful for the connections and communities that inspire me and expand my path.

Sagittarius
11 October 2026

The Aquarius Moon continues, amplifying originality, freedom, and progressive ideas. You may feel restless with routine, craving something new or unconventional. Technology, networking, or exploring visionary ideas could spark breakthroughs. Sagittarius, your adventurous nature thrives when exploring beyond limits—today, embrace opportunities to innovate. The unusual may hold answers you didn't expect. Trust your instinct to wander off the beaten path—it will guide you to wisdom and opportunities unavailable through traditional routes. This is your chance to think big, differently, and boldly.

Gratitude Mantra

I am grateful for my originality and the courage to explore unconventional paths.

Sagittarius
12 October 2026

The Aquarius Moon aligns with Jupiter, your ruling planet, creating expansive, joyful, and inspiring energy. Friendships, group activities, or networking may bring growth opportunities today. Your positivity is magnetic, and people are drawn to your adventurous spirit. Sagittarius, you're reminded that abundance often flows through collaboration and connection. This is a day to celebrate community, to share your fire generously, and to let your optimism ripple outward. When you uplift others, your own light shines even brighter.

Gratitude Mantra

I am grateful for the abundance and joy that flow through connection and community.

Sagittarius
13 October 2026

The Moon moves into Pisces, shifting the energy inward to emotions, intuition, and spiritual reflection. After days of social activity, you may crave solitude or time in peaceful surroundings. Creative and spiritual practices are especially favoured—writing, art, or meditation may bring healing and clarity. Sagittarius, your adventurous soul is reminded that journeys also exist within. Today, stillness brings as much wisdom as exploration. Honour your need for quiet to restore balance and inner peace.

Gratitude Mantra

I am grateful for the peace and wisdom that come from inner reflection.

Sagittarius
14 October 2026

The Pisces Moon continues, amplifying sensitivity and compassion. You may feel more attuned to the emotions of others, making empathy a strength today. Be mindful, however, not to absorb what isn't yours—boundaries protect your energy. Spiritual practices, dreams, or creative outlets may reveal important insights. Sagittarius, your fire is balanced by today's gentle waters. Lean into compassion, but also remember your own needs. True adventure requires both inner healing and outward courage.

Gratitude Mantra

I am grateful for my compassion and the guidance my intuition provides.

Sagittarius
15 October 2026

The Pisces Moon aligns with Neptune, magnifying intuition, imagination, and sensitivity. Your dreams may feel especially vivid, and synchronicities could guide you toward answers you've been seeking. While it may be tempting to escape reality, use this energy for creativity, meditation, or compassion. Sagittarius, you're reminded that not all adventures are external—some are journeys into the unseen. Trust your instincts and embrace inspiration, but avoid making major decisions until clarity returns. Today is about listening more than acting.

Gratitude Mantra

I am grateful for my intuition and the inspiration it brings through quiet, subtle signs.

Sagittarius
16 October 2026

The Moon shifts into Aries, reigniting your fire and enthusiasm. After days of emotional sensitivity, your confidence and boldness return. This is a day for action, fresh starts, and embracing opportunities that excite you. Romance, creativity, or leadership pursuits are favoured, and your charisma draws others toward your energy. Sagittarius, your adventurous spirit is unstoppable under this influence—trust your instincts and take bold steps. Just remember to balance passion with patience for best results.

Gratitude Mantra

I am grateful for my courage to take bold action and the fire that fuels my journey.

Sagittarius
17 October 2026

The Aries Moon continues, boosting your determination and self-expression. You may feel inspired to lead, start a new project, or speak your truth with confidence. Your fire is magnetic, but impatience may surface if others can't keep up with your pace. Sagittarius, this is your chance to show the world your vision, but temper it with awareness. Energy is high, and purposeful action will create long-lasting results. Let your enthusiasm carry you forward, but with focus.

Gratitude Mantra

I am grateful for my passion and the wisdom to channel it into purposeful action.

Sagittarius
18 October 2026

The Aries Moon forms tense aspects, stirring restlessness and impulsive energy. You may feel easily frustrated if progress is delayed or if restrictions hold you back. Instead of reacting sharply, channel this fiery energy into movement—exercise, creative projects, or bold problem-solving. Sagittarius, your challenge today is to balance freedom with responsibility. Harness your energy without letting it spill over recklessly. Growth comes when you master your fire rather than letting it control you.

Gratitude Mantra

I am grateful for my resilience and ability to turn restlessness into growth.

Sagittarius
19 October 2026

The Moon enters Taurus, grounding your energy and slowing the pace. After fiery Aries days, this shift reminds you of the value of patience, stability, and consistency. Practical matters like finances, health, or routines may need attention. Sagittarius, though you prefer adventure, today teaches you that strong foundations support freedom. Savour simple pleasures—good food, nature, or rest. Balance fire with earth energy, and you'll feel both steady and inspired.

Gratitude Mantra

I am grateful for the stability and grounding that support my adventurous spirit.

Sagittarius
20 October 2026

The Taurus Moon continues, encouraging persistence and long-term commitment. Progress may feel slow, but steady steps are building meaningful results. Sagittarius, this is your reminder that adventures are richer when you feel secure. Focus on the practical tasks that ensure your long-term freedom—finances, routines, or health. While not glamorous, today's energy sustains your future dreams. Embrace patience; your fire burns stronger when supported by stability.

Gratitude Mantra

I am grateful for the persistence that builds lasting security and strength.

Sagittarius
21 October 2026

The Taurus Moon aligns with Pluto, intensifying focus and transformation. You may feel compelled to dig deeper into finances, health habits, or personal goals. A breakthrough is possible if you release outdated patterns and commit to empowering changes. Sagittarius, while you prefer speed, transformation requires patience and courage. Today is about laying down stronger foundations that support both your independence and your growth. Trust that what you rebuild now will free you in the long run.

Gratitude Mantra

I am grateful for the transformation that comes from releasing old patterns and embracing empowered choices.

Sagittarius
22 October 2026

The Moon enters Gemini, bringing a lively, curious, and social energy. Conversations may spark inspiration, and networking could open doors to new opportunities. You may feel scattered, juggling multiple ideas or commitments. Sagittarius, this energy excites your adventurous spirit, but remember: not everything deserves your fire. Focus on what aligns with your greater vision. Use today to brainstorm, write, or connect with others—just avoid overcommitting. Inspiration flows freely when curiosity is balanced with discernment.

Gratitude Mantra

I am grateful for my curiosity and the wisdom to focus on what truly excites me.

Sagittarius
23 October 2026

The Gemini Moon continues, keeping your energy light, social, and fast-paced. Opportunities for learning, collaboration, or short trips may arise. Your words carry influence, so communicate with clarity. While your adventurous side loves variety, scattering your focus may leave you drained. Sagittarius, today is about sharing your vision while also listening—sometimes wisdom comes through unexpected voices. Choose quality over quantity in both conversations and commitments. Balance exploration with mindfulness.

Gratitude Mantra

I am grateful for the connections and ideas that expand my horizons with meaning.

Sagittarius
24 October 2026

The Gemini Moon squares Neptune, creating confusion or misunderstandings in communication. You may feel unclear about your next steps or find others misinterpreting your words. Avoid making major commitments or finalising plans until the fog clears. Instead, lean into creativity, writing, or intuitive practices. Sagittarius, this is a reminder to trust your instincts over appearances. Not everything is as it seems today—pause, reflect, and let clarity come naturally. Your optimism will guide you through the haze.

Gratitude Mantra

I am grateful for my patience and the clarity that comes when I trust my instincts.

Sagittarius
25 October 2026

The Moon moves into Cancer, shifting focus to home, family, and emotional security. You may feel more reflective, craving nurturing and connection. This is a day to recharge, spend time with loved ones, or create a safe space for yourself. Old emotions may surface, offering healing if you allow them to flow. Sagittarius, while you love the wide world, your fire also needs a hearth. Today is about tending your inner flame with love and care.

Gratitude Mantra

I am grateful for the love and comfort that restore my spirit and strengthen my journey.

Sagittarius
26 October 2026

The Cancer Moon continues, deepening empathy and intuition. You may sense the emotions of others strongly, which could inspire compassion but also drain your energy if boundaries aren't in place. Creative or spiritual practices bring peace, and time spent near water may be especially healing. Sagittarius, your adventurous soul thrives on movement, yet today the gift is stillness. Inner exploration fuels your outer journeys. Honour your emotional needs alongside your passions.

Gratitude Mantra

I am grateful for my compassion and the healing that comes from honouring my emotional world.

Sagittarius
27 October 2026

The Cancer Moon opposes Pluto, stirring intensity in family or relationship dynamics. Power struggles or unresolved feelings may surface, demanding attention. While this energy feels heavy, it offers transformation if faced with honesty and courage. Sagittarius, you prefer to look forward, but healing sometimes means revisiting the past. Lean into vulnerability—it brings strength. By releasing old wounds, you create space for new beginnings. Today is about cleansing emotional weight so your fire can burn brighter.

Gratitude Mantra

I am grateful for the courage to face emotional intensity and the freedom that healing brings.

Sagittarius
28 October 2026

The Moon enters Leo, lifting your energy with confidence, joy, and creativity. After emotional days, you're ready to shine again. This is a wonderful time for self-expression, romance, or leadership. Your charisma is magnetic, drawing opportunities and admiration. Sagittarius, your adventurous fire thrives under this influence—live boldly, follow passions, and share your light generously. Today is about celebrating who you are and inspiring others to embrace their own uniqueness.

Gratitude Mantra

I am grateful for my confidence and the joy of living authentically.

Sagittarius
29 October 2026

The Leo Moon continues, filling the day with confidence, playfulness, and self-expression. You may feel eager to step into the spotlight, whether through creative projects, romance, or social settings. Your charisma is magnetic, drawing people toward you. Sagittarius, your adventurous spirit thrives under this influence—you're encouraged to live boldly, follow your passions, and enjoy life's pleasures without hesitation. Just remember to balance your fire with humility. True leadership isn't only about shining—it's about inspiring others to shine too.

Gratitude Mantra

I am grateful for my courage to live boldly and the joy I inspire in others.

Sagittarius
30 October 2026

The Leo Moon aligns with Jupiter, your ruling planet, amplifying joy, optimism, and abundance. Opportunities may appear in love, creativity, or social connections, and your confidence is sky-high. This is one of those days when everything feels possible. Sagittarius, lean into experiences that bring laughter, adventure, and expansion. Your fire is magnetic, and the more you share your light, the more blessings return to you. Say yes to what excites your spirit—it's the universe affirming your path.

Gratitude Mantra

I am grateful for the abundance and joy that flow when I follow my passions wholeheartedly.

Sagittarius
31 October 2026

The Moon shifts into Virgo, grounding fiery energy and turning focus toward details, organisation, and responsibilities. After days of expansive energy, it's time to refine your plans and create structure. Practical matters such as health, finances, or routines benefit from your attention now. Sagittarius, you may not love the slower pace, but this energy ensures your freedom is sustainable. Think of today as sharpening your tools—you're preparing for bigger adventures. Progress comes through focus and patience.

Gratitude Mantra

I am grateful for the clarity and grounding that help me build strong foundations.

November 2026

Sagittarius
01 November 2026

The Virgo Moon continues, encouraging productivity and self-improvement. You may feel motivated to refine habits, streamline routines, or resolve lingering issues. Perfectionism could surface, but remember that progress is more important than flawless results. Sagittarius, your gift lies in seeing the big picture, but today you're reminded of the value of details. Small steps create long-term change. Honour the process and trust that each effort is building momentum for future success.

Gratitude Mantra

I am grateful for the progress that comes from small, consistent actions.

Sagittarius
02 November 2026

The Virgo Moon aligns with Uranus, shaking up routines with unexpected changes or fresh insights. While disruptions may feel inconvenient, they hold the key to breakthroughs. Sagittarius, your adventurous fire thrives on surprises—embrace today's shake-ups as opportunities for growth. A new perspective or approach could simplify a long-standing problem. Stay adaptable and curious; the cosmos is inviting you to innovate. What feels like a disruption may become the turning point you've been waiting for.

Gratitude Mantra

I am grateful for the breakthroughs that come through flexibility and openness to change.

Sagittarius
03 November 2026

The Moon moves into Libra, shifting attention toward relationships, balance, and harmony. Partnerships—romantic, professional, or social—take centre stage today. Cooperation and compromise are favoured, but don't lose your authentic voice in the process. Sagittarius, you love independence, but relationships help you expand in ways solo journeys cannot. Seek harmony while honouring your truth. This is a day to build bridges, resolve conflicts, and strengthen bonds through empathy, honesty, and balance.

Gratitude Mantra

I am grateful for the harmony and balance that enrich my relationships.

Sagittarius
04 November 2026

The Libra Moon continues, highlighting diplomacy, fairness, and collaboration. You may feel called to mediate, support others, or engage in partnerships that spark creativity and growth. Your natural optimism makes you an inspiring presence in group settings. Sagittarius, today's energy asks you to soften your truth with compassion. Speak honestly, but with awareness of how your words land. When you combine boldness with kindness, you create connections that uplift everyone involved.

Gratitude Mantra

I am grateful for my ability to speak truth with compassion and create harmony.

Sagittarius
05 November 2026

The Libra Moon aligns with Pluto, stirring intensity in partnerships or social dynamics. You may feel compelled to address hidden truths or power imbalances in relationships. While conversations may feel heavy, they carry potential for deep healing. Sagittarius, your gift of honesty can be transformative when paired with compassion. Use today to rebuild trust, strengthen bonds, or release connections that no longer align with your growth. Depth may feel challenging, but it creates freedom.

Gratitude Mantra

I am grateful for the courage to face truths and the healing it brings to my relationships.

Sagittarius
06 November 2026

The Moon shifts into Scorpio, amplifying intuition, passion, and emotional depth. You may feel drawn to introspection, spiritual practices, or exploring life's mysteries. Scorpio energy asks you to look beneath the surface, uncovering truths that can no longer be ignored. Sagittarius, though you prefer the lightness of adventure, today's gift is found in depth. Transformation comes when you're brave enough to explore your shadows. Journaling, meditation, or honest conversations may bring breakthroughs.

Gratitude Mantra

I am grateful for my willingness to dive deep and the transformation that follows.

Sagittarius
07 November 2026

The Scorpio Moon continues, intensifying themes of trust, intimacy, and emotional release. You may feel magnetic yet vulnerable, as hidden issues in relationships or finances surface. While this can feel uncomfortable, it's a chance to reset and transform. Sagittarius, your optimism helps you approach challenges with courage. Face what arises directly, and you'll create space for deeper bonds and new opportunities. Remember—freedom often comes through letting go of what weighs you down.

Gratitude Mantra

I am grateful for the strength to release old burdens and embrace transformation.

Sagittarius
08 November 2026

The Scorpio Moon aligns with Neptune, heightening intuition, dreams, and creative inspiration. Emotions may feel intense, but there's also a softness to the energy that encourages healing and compassion. Spiritual practices, artistic outlets, or time in solitude will be deeply restorative. Sagittarius, while your nature is fiery, today invites you into water's realm of flow and imagination. Surrender control and allow inspiration to move through you—you'll find clarity in unexpected ways.

Gratitude Mantra

I am grateful for my intuition and the inspiration that flows when I surrender to the moment.

Sagittarius
09 November 2026

The Moon enters Sagittarius, lifting your energy and reigniting your adventurous fire. After days of emotional depth, you're ready to expand, explore, and laugh again. Confidence and optimism surge, and opportunities may come through travel, learning, or spontaneous encounters. This is your natural rhythm, Sagittarius—following curiosity and living boldly. Say yes to experiences that excite your spirit. The cosmos is encouraging you to celebrate your uniqueness and let your fire inspire others.

Gratitude Mantra

I am grateful for my adventurous spirit and the opportunities it brings.

Sagittarius
10 November 2026

The Sagittarius Moon continues, amplifying your charisma, confidence, and zest for life. This is a day to pursue personal goals, speak your truth, or embark on new adventures. Your enthusiasm attracts opportunities, but be mindful not to scatter your energy across too many directions. Sagittarius, your power lies in aligning your fire with purpose. When you focus your passion, you can achieve incredible progress. Today is about stepping boldly into opportunities that match your vision.

Gratitude Mantra

I am grateful for my confidence and the focus that channels my fire into purposeful action.

Sagittarius
11 November 2026

The Sagittarius Moon aligns with Jupiter, your ruling planet, blessing you with luck, growth, and expansion. Opportunities may flow easily—through learning, travel, or chance encounters—and your adventurous spirit is ready to embrace them. This is one of those days where the universe feels aligned in your favour. Sagittarius, your optimism is your magnet—share your vision boldly and trust that abundance will follow. Celebrate this wave of expansion by stepping into possibilities with joy.

Gratitude Mantra

I am grateful for the abundance and growth that come when I follow my adventurous heart.

Sagittarius
12 November 2026

The Moon shifts into Capricorn, grounding your fiery energy and redirecting it toward structure and responsibility. After expansive Sagittarius days, this influence may feel heavier, but it's necessary for balance. Focus on career, finances, or long-term goals that require discipline. Sagittarius, you thrive on freedom, but freedom is strongest when supported by stability. Today asks you to commit to the small steps that create security for future adventures. Progress may feel slower, but it's deeply meaningful.

Gratitude Mantra

I am grateful for the discipline and structure that sustain my freedom.

Sagittarius
13 November 2026

The Capricorn Moon continues, emphasising perseverance and productivity. You may be called to step into leadership or prove your reliability in work or personal matters. Recognition from authority figures is possible, but more importantly, you'll feel pride in your steady progress. Sagittarius, though you prefer fast leaps, today's lesson is that success is built brick by brick. Your adventurous fire is stronger when grounded in consistency—trust that effort now supports freedom later.

Gratitude Mantra

I am grateful for the persistence and reliability that strengthen my foundation.

Sagittarius
14 November 2026

The Capricorn Moon aligns with Uranus, bringing unexpected changes in routines or responsibilities. Disruptions may feel inconvenient, but they carry opportunities to refresh old patterns or find better solutions. Sagittarius, your adaptability is a gift—today it helps you turn surprises into breakthroughs. Instead of resisting change, flow with it. What feels like a detour may actually be a shortcut to progress. The cosmos is reminding you that freedom often comes through flexibility.

Gratitude Mantra

I am grateful for my adaptability and the breakthroughs that change brings.

Sagittarius
15 November 2026

The Moon enters Aquarius, turning your attention toward friendships, collaboration, and visionary ideas. You may feel energised by conversations with like-minded people or inspired to contribute to causes bigger than yourself. Sagittarius, your adventurous nature thrives in groups that expand your worldview. Today is about sharing your fire and learning from collective wisdom. Connections made now may open unexpected doors. Celebrate the power of community—it magnifies your light and broadens your path.

Gratitude Mantra

I am grateful for the friendships and collaborations that inspire and expand my journey.

Sagittarius
16 November 2026

The Aquarius Moon continues, amplifying originality, curiosity, and freedom. Routine may feel dull, and you'll crave excitement or unconventional experiences. Technology, networking, or innovative thinking could spark breakthroughs. Sagittarius, you're reminded that adventure isn't always physical—it can be intellectual or social too. Follow your curiosity into new territory, even if it feels unusual. The more you embrace originality, the more aligned your path becomes. Today is about exploration beyond the ordinary.

Gratitude Mantra

I am grateful for my originality and the courage to explore new ways of living.

Sagittarius
17 November 2026

The Aquarius Moon aligns with Jupiter, boosting optimism, charm, and inspiration. Opportunities may arise through friendships, groups, or unexpected conversations. Sagittarius, your positivity is magnetic today—share your ideas boldly and let your adventurous spirit ripple through the collective. The cosmos reminds you that abundance flows through connection as much as independence. Collaboration can carry you further than solo pursuits now. Open your heart to the support available—you don't have to do everything alone.

Gratitude Mantra

I am grateful for the abundance and joy that come through community and connection.

Sagittarius
18 November 2026

The Moon shifts into Pisces, softening the pace and drawing your focus inward. Emotions, creativity, and intuition feel heightened. You may crave solitude, peace, or nurturing connections. Spiritual practices, art, or time in nature can be especially healing. Sagittarius, though you love movement, the universe reminds you that rest is part of growth. Honour your emotional needs and allow yourself to restore. The inner journey today is as valuable as outer adventures.

Gratitude Mantra

I am grateful for the peace and wisdom that flow from rest and inner reflection.

Sagittarius
19 November 2026

The Pisces Moon continues, heightening intuition, compassion, and imagination. You may feel more sensitive to others' emotions, making empathy a gift but also a potential drain if boundaries aren't set. Creative and spiritual pursuits flourish—journaling, painting, or meditation may offer clarity. Sagittarius, your adventurous soul often seeks truth in the external world, but today's wisdom comes from within. Don't underestimate the power of inner exploration—it fuels your fire for the journeys ahead.

Gratitude Mantra

I am grateful for my compassion and the wisdom that arises from inner exploration.

Sagittarius
20 November 2026

The Pisces Moon harmonises with Pluto, creating opportunities for deep emotional healing and transformation. Old wounds or lingering fears may surface, but instead of resisting, lean into them with honesty. By releasing the weight of the past, you make room for renewal. Sagittarius, though you prefer to keep moving forward, true freedom sometimes requires looking back. Today invites you to embrace vulnerability, trust the process, and step into a lighter, freer version of yourself.

Gratitude Mantra

I am grateful for the healing that comes when I release the past with honesty and courage.

Sagittarius
21 November 2026

The Moon enters Aries, sparking boldness, confidence, and action. After days of introspection, you're ready to move forward with energy and enthusiasm. This is a great time to start a new project, pursue passion, or take initiative in love or career. Sagittarius, this fiery influence resonates with your adventurous nature—you're unstoppable when courage and instinct align. Don't hold back, but remember to pace yourself. Progress comes through focused action, not scattered bursts of energy.

Gratitude Mantra

I am grateful for my courage to act boldly and the focus that drives me forward.

Sagittarius
22 November 2026

The Aries Moon continues, amplifying your leadership and magnetism. People are drawn to your fire, and opportunities may arise to showcase your vision or inspire others. Confidence is high, but be mindful of impatience—others may not move as quickly as you. Sagittarius, this is a day to take charge but also to empower those around you. Leadership shines brightest when it uplifts as well as directs. Use your passion to spark collective progress.

Gratitude Mantra

I am grateful for my ability to inspire and lead with authenticity.

Sagittarius
23 November 2026

The Aries Moon forms tense aspects, stirring restlessness and impulsive tendencies. You may feel frustrated if things don't move quickly enough, leading to hasty words or actions. Instead of reacting, channel this fiery energy into physical activity, problem-solving, or creative pursuits. Sagittarius, you love freedom, but today's lesson is patience—sometimes slowing down brings more progress than rushing. Balance fire with wisdom, and you'll find clarity and strength where frustration once lived.

Gratitude Mantra

I am grateful for my resilience and ability to turn restlessness into purposeful action.

Sagittarius
24 November 2026

The Moon moves into Taurus, grounding your energy and shifting focus toward stability, comfort, and practical matters. This is a day for tending to finances, health, or routines that bring security. After fiery Aries days, the cosmos asks you to slow down and find balance. Sagittarius, though you thrive on adventure, grounding sustains your freedom. Enjoy simple pleasures today—nature, food, or connection with loved ones. Balance fire with earth for true strength.

Gratitude Mantra

I am grateful for the stability and grounding that support my adventurous life.

Sagittarius
25 November 2026

The Taurus Moon continues, encouraging persistence, patience, and steady effort. Progress may feel slow, but don't mistake it for stagnation—each step builds lasting results. This is a perfect day for financial planning, health improvements, or solidifying long-term goals. Sagittarius, though you love speed, today teaches you that consistency sustains freedom. The slow burn creates the strongest flame. Trust the process—it's carrying you exactly where you need to go.

Gratitude Mantra

I am grateful for the patience and consistency that build lasting success.

Sagittarius
26 November 2026

The Taurus Moon aligns with Saturn, highlighting discipline, persistence, and responsibility. You may feel motivated to focus on financial planning, career stability, or commitments that require long-term effort. While the energy feels steady rather than fast, it brings satisfaction through progress. Sagittarius, your adventurous spirit may resist structure, but today's grounding energy ensures your freedom lasts. Think of it as building scaffolding for your dreams. Patience, planning, and effort today secure tomorrow's opportunities.

Gratitude Mantra

I am grateful for the discipline and patience that strengthen the foundations of my dreams.

Sagittarius
27 November 2026

The Moon enters Gemini, sparking curiosity, conversation, and variety. You may feel pulled in many directions—social invitations, ideas, or projects competing for your attention. While this energy excites you, scattering your focus could lead to burnout. Sagittarius, your challenge today is discernment—choose what aligns with your vision and let go of distractions. Communication flows easily, making it a good day for writing, networking, or brainstorming. Inspiration surrounds you—focus it wisely.

Gratitude Mantra

I am grateful for my curiosity and the wisdom to focus on what truly matters.

Sagittarius
28 November 2026

The Gemini Moon continues, keeping life fast-paced and lively. You may feel restless, eager for change, or open to new experiences. While variety excites you, balance it with purpose. Sagittarius, your adventurous fire can scatter if spread too thin—today asks you to channel it. Conversations and connections may spark new ideas or unexpected opportunities. Stay curious, but remain grounded enough to recognise which doors are worth walking through. Inspiration flows best with focus.

Gratitude Mantra

I am grateful for my curiosity and the focus that turns ideas into opportunities.

Sagittarius
29 November 2026

The Gemini Moon squares Neptune, creating confusion or miscommunication. Plans may shift, or clarity may feel out of reach. Instead of forcing answers, lean into creativity, intuition, or rest. Sagittarius, your optimism helps you navigate uncertainty, but don't rush decisions today—clarity will come later. Use the dreamy energy for journaling, art, or meditation. What feels unclear now may reveal itself in unexpected ways. Sometimes the path forward is revealed through stillness, not action.

Gratitude Mantra

I am grateful for my patience and trust that clarity will come in its own time.

Sagittarius
30 November 2026

The Moon moves into Cancer, turning focus toward home, family, and emotional nourishment. You may crave comfort, safety, or connection with loved ones. Old feelings could surface, offering chances for healing. Sagittarius, while you thrive on adventure, you also need grounding in love and belonging. Today's cosmic invitation is to nurture your inner world, recharge your spirit, and honour the emotional foundations that make your fire sustainable. Adventure begins at home, within the heart.

Gratitude Mantra

I am grateful for the love and comfort that ground me and fuel my spirit.

December 2026

Sagittarius
01 December 2026

The Cancer Moon continues, heightening sensitivity and intuition. You may feel more empathetic, making it easier to connect with others deeply. Be mindful, however, not to carry burdens that aren't yours—boundaries protect your energy. Creative and spiritual practices are favoured today. Sagittarius, you often look outward for answers, but today the universe asks you to look inward. Stillness, reflection, and emotional honesty bring the guidance you seek. Honour your inner compass—it won't fail you.

Gratitude Mantra

I am grateful for my intuition and the clarity it brings when I listen inwardly.

Sagittarius
02 December 2026

The Cancer Moon opposes Pluto, stirring intensity in family or relationship matters. Emotions may run deep, and power struggles could arise. While uncomfortable, these moments carry the potential for transformation. Sagittarius, your gift is optimism—use it to face challenges with courage and perspective. By embracing honesty and releasing old emotional weight, you free yourself for future adventures. Today's energy is about cleansing and renewal—face it bravely, and you'll emerge lighter and stronger.

Gratitude Mantra

I am grateful for my courage to face intensity and the freedom that comes from release.

Sagittarius
03 December 2026

The Moon enters Leo, reigniting your fire and confidence. After emotional Cancer days, you're ready to shine again—boldly, joyfully, and unapologetically. Creativity, romance, and leadership opportunities are favoured. Sagittarius, your adventurous nature thrives under Leo's warmth, and today you'll feel the pull to celebrate life and embrace passions. Share your vision openly—your charisma attracts admiration and support. Be mindful not to dominate; inspire others to shine alongside you. Your fire is brightest when shared generously.

Gratitude Mantra

I am grateful for my confidence and the joy of sharing my light with others.

Sagittarius
04 December 2026

The Leo Moon continues, amplifying playfulness, courage, and self-expression. Opportunities for romance, socialising, or creative projects may arise. Your adventurous spirit loves this energy—it feels like the universe is encouraging you to live fully. Sagittarius, while it's tempting to say yes to everything, choose what truly excites your soul. Focused joy is more fulfilling than scattered attention. Lead boldly, laugh loudly, and let your energy ripple outward—it will inspire everyone you encounter.

Gratitude Mantra

I am grateful for the joy that fills my life when I follow what excites me.

Sagittarius
05 December 2026

The Leo Moon aligns with Jupiter, your ruling planet, blessing you with optimism, luck, and expansion. This is a day where everything feels possible—romance, creativity, travel, or social opportunities may come easily. Sagittarius, your adventurous fire blazes brightly now, attracting abundance and joy. Be bold in your choices and generous with your spirit. The cosmos is amplifying your natural magnetism—say yes to experiences that expand your heart and horizons. Trust that abundance flows when you live authentically.

Gratitude Mantra

I am grateful for the abundance that flows when I live boldly and authentically.

Sagittarius
06 December 2026

The Moon enters Virgo, grounding fiery energy and redirecting your focus toward details, routines, and responsibilities. After expansive Leo days, the cosmos asks you to refine and organise. Work, health, or financial matters may benefit from practical attention. Sagittarius, you may not love the slower pace, but it ensures your freedom lasts. Think of today as strengthening the foundation beneath your adventures. Small, precise steps carry you toward your dreams. Balance fire with patience for lasting results.

Gratitude Mantra

I am grateful for the clarity and discipline that support my long-term freedom.

Sagittarius
07 December 2026

The Virgo Moon continues, encouraging productivity and problem-solving. You may feel motivated to refine habits or complete tasks you've been avoiding. While perfectionism could creep in, remind yourself that progress matters more than flawlessness. Sagittarius, your gift is seeing the big picture, but today the details matter. Honour both perspectives—vision and execution. The satisfaction of completing small steps today fuels your confidence for future adventures. Trust the process, even when it feels ordinary.

Gratitude Mantra

I am grateful for the progress that comes from steady, thoughtful effort.

Sagittarius
08 December 2026

The Virgo Moon aligns with Uranus, bringing unexpected shifts in routines or responsibilities. Disruptions may initially frustrate you, but they carry opportunities for innovation. Sagittarius, you thrive on adaptability—today's surprises may spark creative solutions or fresh approaches. Don't resist change; embrace it as an invitation to grow. What seems inconvenient now may prove to be the breakthrough you've been waiting for. Trust the universe's timing—it often knows better than your plans.

Gratitude Mantra

I am grateful for my flexibility and the breakthroughs that come from change.

Sagittarius
09 December 2026

The Moon moves into Libra, turning attention toward relationships, partnerships, and balance. Harmony and diplomacy are favoured, making it a good day to collaborate, mediate, or reconnect with loved ones. Sagittarius, while you treasure independence, relationships enrich your growth. Seek balance between freedom and connection. Compromise today does not mean sacrificing your truth—it's about finding harmony where differences exist. Authentic collaboration can lead to expansion, both personally and professionally. Honour the value of shared journeys.

Gratitude Mantra

I am grateful for the harmony and balance that strengthen my connections.

Sagittarius
10 December 2026

The Libra Moon continues, encouraging balance, fairness, and connection. Relationships may feel highlighted, with opportunities to collaborate or resolve lingering tensions. Your natural optimism makes you a peacemaker, Sagittarius, but remember to honour your truth as well. Today is about harmony without self-sacrifice. Whether in love, friendship, or work, diplomacy and compassion will bring positive outcomes. When you balance independence with cooperation, your relationships become not a burden, but a source of expansion.

Gratitude Mantra

I am grateful for the balance between independence and connection that strengthens my path.

Sagittarius
11 December 2026

The Libra Moon squares Pluto, stirring emotional intensity in partnerships. Power struggles or buried feelings may surface, demanding honesty. While this can feel uncomfortable, it is an opportunity for transformation. Sagittarius, your gift of truth-telling can heal when delivered with compassion. Lean into vulnerability—by facing challenges directly, you create freedom for yourself and deeper bonds with others. Today's intensity clears away what no longer serves your highest growth.

Gratitude Mantra

I am grateful for the courage to embrace honesty and the freedom it brings in my relationships.

Sagittarius
12 December 2026

The Moon enters Scorpio, deepening your emotions and sharpening intuition. You may feel drawn to inner reflection, uncovering truths or healing old wounds. This is a day for transformation, not surface-level fixes. Sagittarius, though you prefer the lightness of adventure, today's energy asks you to explore depth. Growth lies in facing shadows with courage. Journaling, meditation, or heartfelt conversations can bring breakthroughs. Trust that intensity leads to empowerment when embraced, not avoided.

Gratitude Mantra

I am grateful for my courage to face depth and the transformation it brings.

Sagittarius
13 December 2026

The Scorpio Moon continues, intensifying themes of trust, intimacy, and release. Relationships may feel magnetic, yet demanding, as hidden dynamics come to light. Financial or shared resource matters may also surface. Sagittarius, while this energy can feel heavy, it allows you to grow through honesty and courage. Today, transformation occurs by letting go of what no longer supports your truth. Release resistance—it's the gateway to renewal. Remember, freedom is born from shedding old weights.

Gratitude Mantra

I am grateful for the strength to release what no longer serves me.

Sagittarius
14 December 2026

The Scorpio Moon aligns with Neptune, enhancing intuition, creativity, and compassion. You may feel inspired to dream, create, or connect spiritually. While emotions may run deep, they are softened by imagination and empathy. Sagittarius, this is a day to embrace your inner visionary—explore art, meditation, or soulful conversations. You're reminded that adventure exists in the mystical as much as in the physical world. Trust intuitive nudges; they're guiding you toward clarity and healing.

Gratitude Mantra

I am grateful for my intuition and the creative inspiration that flows through me.

Sagittarius
15 December 2026

The Moon shifts into Sagittarius, amplifying optimism, fire, and freedom. This is your cosmic reset, a chance to embrace new adventures and live boldly. Opportunities may come through travel, learning, or chance encounters. Confidence surges, and your charisma shines brightly. Sagittarius, this is your element—lean into your truth and trust your instincts. Today, the universe invites you to celebrate your individuality and inspire others with your passion for life. Say yes to what excites your spirit.

Gratitude Mantra

I am grateful for my adventurous fire and the opportunities it attracts.

Sagittarius
16 December 2026

The Sagittarius Moon continues, strengthening confidence, joy, and expansion. This is a perfect day to set intentions, share your vision, or take bold steps toward personal goals. Your optimism is magnetic, drawing support and opportunities. Sagittarius, your challenge is not to scatter your energy but to channel it purposefully. When your adventurous fire is guided by focus, you become unstoppable. Embrace the freedom to explore while keeping your eye on what truly matters.

Gratitude Mantra

I am grateful for my confidence and the focus that fuels my adventurous path.

Sagittarius
17 December 2026

The Sagittarius Moon aligns with Jupiter, your ruling planet, creating a wave of optimism, luck, and expansion. This is one of those golden days when opportunities seem to fall into your lap—through travel, study, or meaningful connections. Your adventurous fire blazes brighter than usual, inspiring others as much as yourself. Sagittarius, embrace bold choices and step into possibilities that excite you. When you follow joy, abundance naturally follows. Trust your instincts—they're aligned with cosmic support today.

Gratitude Mantra

I am grateful for the abundance and joy that flow when I follow my adventurous heart.

Sagittarius
18 December 2026

The Moon shifts into Capricorn, grounding fiery energy and focusing on long-term goals. After days of expansion, this is your moment to solidify progress with structure and persistence. Career, finances, or health routines benefit from attention now. Sagittarius, though you prefer freedom over discipline, today shows you that true independence is built on strong foundations. Steady effort will secure your future adventures. Honour this energy—it helps turn big dreams into achievable realities.

Gratitude Mantra

I am grateful for the discipline that builds a strong foundation for my freedom.

Sagittarius
19 December 2026

The Capricorn Moon continues, reminding you that persistence leads to success. You may feel called to prove your reliability or commit to responsibilities that ensure stability. Recognition from authority figures or mentors is possible. Sagittarius, though routine may feel restrictive, this is the kind of work that creates lasting rewards. Each small step now is part of the bigger picture of your adventurous life. Patience today becomes freedom tomorrow—embrace the process with pride.

Gratitude Mantra

I am grateful for my persistence and the progress it creates.

Sagittarius
20 December 2026

The Capricorn Moon aligns with Uranus, bringing sudden shifts to routines or responsibilities. Disruptions may feel frustrating at first, but they open the door to innovative solutions. Sagittarius, you thrive when life surprises you—today's changes may actually refresh your perspective. Stay flexible and see what new opportunities emerge from the shake-up. The cosmos is nudging you to adapt and grow. Trust that what feels inconvenient now may lead to greater freedom later.

Gratitude Mantra

I am grateful for my flexibility and the new opportunities that change brings.

Sagittarius
21 December 2026

The Moon enters Aquarius, sparking originality, community, and curiosity. Friendships, collaborations, and networking may bring inspiration or opportunities. Your adventurous spirit thrives when surrounded by like-minded people who expand your perspective. Sagittarius, today reminds you that growth multiplies when shared. Don't isolate—share your light and ideas with others. Collective energy fuels your fire and opens doors you couldn't reach alone. Be open, curious, and ready for conversations that inspire fresh directions.

Gratitude Mantra

I am grateful for the connections and collaborations that expand my journey.

Sagittarius
22 December 2026

The Aquarius Moon continues, amplifying your need for freedom and originality. You may feel restless with routine and crave excitement or unconventional approaches. Sagittarius, this is your reminder that exploration doesn't always require physical travel—it can be mental, social, or spiritual. Follow your curiosity into new territory. Break away from old patterns, embrace innovation, and let your adventurous fire guide you. Today is about thinking bigger and differently—don't limit yourself to tradition.

Gratitude Mantra

I am grateful for my originality and the freedom to explore new possibilities.

Sagittarius
23 December 2026

The Aquarius Moon aligns with Jupiter, bringing joy, optimism, and collective growth. Opportunities may come through friendships, groups, or spontaneous encounters. Your positivity is magnetic, and your vision has the power to inspire many. Sagittarius, the cosmos is reminding you that you don't have to walk your path alone—collaboration will carry you further. Today is about celebrating community, generosity, and shared wisdom. When you share your fire, it spreads like wildfire in the best way.

Gratitude Mantra

I am grateful for the abundance and joy that flow through community and shared vision.

Sagittarius
24 December 2026

The Moon moves into Pisces, softening the energy and pulling your focus inward. After the social buzz of Aquarius, today asks for rest, reflection, and emotional care. Creativity, spirituality, or time near water may feel particularly nourishing. Sagittarius, your adventurous spirit thrives on motion, but today the journey is inward. Trust your intuition, honour your emotions, and allow space for gentle healing. This is a perfect day to recharge before stepping into festive celebrations.

Gratitude Mantra

I am grateful for the peace and wisdom that flow when I honour stillness and reflection.

Sagittarius
25 December 2026

The Pisces Moon continues, making this Christmas Day a time of compassion, imagination, and soulful connection. Emotions may run deep, but they also inspire generosity and warmth. Sagittarius, your natural optimism blends beautifully with this energy—you may find joy in giving, storytelling, or simply being present with loved ones. The cosmos encourages you to soften, to appreciate quiet blessings, and to celebrate the heart rather than the hustle.

Gratitude Mantra

I am grateful for the love, generosity, and soulful connections that make this day meaningful.

Sagittarius
26 December 2026

The Pisces Moon aligns with Pluto, intensifying emotions and highlighting themes of release and renewal. You may feel reflective about the year gone by, considering what to carry forward and what to leave behind. Sagittarius, while you love to look ahead, today is about closure. Allow yourself to honour both endings and beginnings. Emotional release now creates space for the adventures awaiting you in the year to come. Transformation is the gift of today's energy.

Gratitude Mantra

I am grateful for the release of old weights and the space created for new adventures.

Sagittarius
27 December 2026

The Moon enters Aries, reigniting your fire and confidence. After reflective Pisces days, you're ready to move forward with passion and purpose. This is a great time for setting intentions, starting a project, or simply embracing adventure. Sagittarius, this energy resonates with your truth—bold, direct, and enthusiastic. The universe encourages you to step into the new with courage. Don't hesitate; follow your instincts and ignite the path forward.

Gratitude Mantra

I am grateful for my courage to take bold steps and embrace fresh beginnings.

Sagittarius
28 December 2026

The Aries Moon continues, amplifying leadership, drive, and passion. Your adventurous spirit feels unstoppable today—you're inspired to act, connect, and create momentum. Be mindful, however, of impatience; not everyone moves at your pace. Sagittarius, your fire shines brightest when tempered with awareness. Channel this energy into purposeful action, and you'll accomplish more than expected. Today is about embracing your boldness while inspiring others through example rather than force.

Gratitude Mantra

I am grateful for my passion and the focus that guides it toward meaningful action.

Sagittarius
29 December 2026

The Aries Moon forms tense aspects, stirring restlessness and impulsive energy. You may feel frustrated if plans stall or people slow you down. Instead of reacting harshly, direct your fire into physical activity, problem-solving, or creative outlets. Sagittarius, your challenge today is to use intensity constructively. Impatience can either spark mistakes or fuel breakthroughs—it's your choice. By channelling energy with awareness, you'll find clarity where frustration once lived.

Gratitude Mantra

I am grateful for my resilience and ability to turn frustration into growth.

Sagittarius
30 December 2026

The Moon enters Taurus, grounding your energy and slowing the pace. After fiery Aries days, today asks you to focus on stability, comfort, and simple pleasures. Practical matters like finances, routines, or health may require attention. Sagittarius, though you prefer movement, grounding sustains your freedom. Nature, good food, or time with loved ones will feel deeply restorative. This steady energy is the pause you need before the year closes.

Gratitude Mantra

I am grateful for the grounding and comfort that restore my energy.

Sagittarius
31 December 2026

The Taurus Moon continues, making New Year's Eve a time to reflect on stability, gratitude, and the foundations you've built. While celebrations may call, you may also crave simplicity—choosing meaningful connections over noisy distractions. Sagittarius, the cosmos asks you to honour how far you've come and set intentions for the adventures ahead. Balance celebration with reflection, and step into the new year grounded, grateful, and ready to expand.

Gratitude Mantra

I am grateful for the lessons of this year and the adventures awaiting me in the next.

www.ingramcontent.com/pod-product-compliance
Lightning Source LLC
Chambersburg PA
CBHW071146070526
44584CB00019B/2672